Isabel's journey is one of beauty and strength. She is vulnerable, thoughtful and thought-provoking. This is a book every girl who longs to know God should have.

—Marguerite P Sigafus
MA Former LPC, Editor

Isabel begs the question of what does a life fully surrendered to God look like. In this book, she dissects and categorizes just that. With illuminating questions at the end of the chapters, Inner Beauty becomes more than a book. It becomes a personal journey to achieve a life surrendered to our own true inner beauty. Mrs. McCoy has created an effective structure for a dynamic devotional. I highly recommend this book to anyone who's not afraid to look in the mirror.

—Dr. Deborah Darling
Prophet and International minister

Inner Beauty

GOODBYE self-rejection
and
HELLO self-love
beyond the mirror

Isabel Perez-McCoy

Inner Beauty
Copyright © 2019 Isabel Perez-McCoy
Published by She Proclaims, an imprint of Ear to Hear Publishing LLC
4741 Central St. Ste 472
Kansas City, MO 64112

ISBN 978-0-9861935-6-9 ▪ eBook ISBN: 978-0-9861935-7-6

Unless otherwise indicated, all Scripture quotations are taken from the New King James Version®. Copyright © 1982 by Thomas Nelson, Inc.

Scripture quotations marked AMP are taken from the Amplified® Bible. Copyright © 2015 by The Lockman Foundation. Used by permission. www.Lockman.org

Scripture quotations marked CEV are taken from the Contemporary English Version. Copyright © 1991, 1992, 1995 by American Bible Society. Used by permission.

Scripture quotations marked ESV® are taken from the ESV Bible (The Holy Bible, English Standard Version®), copyright © 2001 by Crossway, a publishing ministry of Good News Publishers. Used by permission. All rights reserved.

Scripture quotations marked ISV are taken from the Holy Bible: International Standard Version®. Copyright © 1996-forever by The ISV Foundation. ALL RIGHTS RESERVED INTERNATIONALLY. Used by permission.

Scripture quotations marked NASB are taken from the New American Standard Bible®. Copyright © 1960, 1962, 1963, 1968, 1971, 1972, 1973, 1975, 1977, 1995 by The Lockman Foundation. Used by permission. www.Lockman.org

Scripture quotations marked NIV are taken from THE HOLY BIBLE, NEW INTERNATIONAL VERSION®, NIV®. Copyright © 1973, 1978, 1984, 2011 by Biblica, Inc.® Used by permission. All rights reserved worldwide.

Scripture quotations marked NHEB are taken from the New Heart English Bible® is not copyrighted and is dedicated to the Public Domain by the editors and translators.

Printed in the United States of America

Library of Congress Control Number: 2019909196

No part of this book may be reproduced or transmitted in any form or by any means, electronic or mechanical, including photocopying and recording, or by any information storage or retrieval system, except as may be expressly permitted in writing by the publisher. This book is protected by the copyright laws of the United States of America. Requests for permission should be addressed in writing to Ear to Hear Publishing™ LLC 4741 Central St. Ste 472 Kansas City, MO 64112 or visit www.eartohearbooks.com or 816-287-0532.

Dedications...

I'd like to dedicate this book to all the beautiful women and girls in my family: my mother, Esperanza; my daughters, Khiarra and Jessica; my sister, Sandy, and my sister-in-law, Jodi; my nieces, Monique, Jazzmine, Eileen, Alyssa, Lily, Joy and Nicole; and my great nieces, Ivorie and Aubrey.

The world teaches young girls that beauty is how good you look on the outside.
Let's teach our daughters that real beauty is being kind.
That real beauty is purity of the heart.
That real beauty is loving Jesus and loving our neighbor.
That real beauty is who we are and not what we see.
—Khiarra Vasquez

Acknowledgments...

First I would like to give thanks to God my heavenly Father for giving me the inspiration, courage and grace to write this book. Without Him I can do nothing, but with Him I can do all things.

To my husband, Merrill, thank you for being so patient and so gracious with me and for praying and supporting me during the seasons of writing and during the process of this book being published.

To my beautiful daughter Khiarra, thank you so much for loving me in my weaknesses, helping me at home, creating Facebook content, and being patient with me on those very busy days.

To my best friend Penny, thank you for laughs, fun and listening to me. I know without a doubt God brought you into my life when I needed it the most.

To the beautiful older women God has given me the privilege to serve and take care of and that demonstrated true Inner Beauty. Thank you Mrs. Barbara Unruh, Ms. Hilda

Heikkinen, Mrs. Joanne Farris and Mrs. Shirley Gottstein.

To Mr. Fred Farris, who encouraged and inspired me to write, thank you so much for all your writing tips, suggestions, and expertise.

To my mentors, Joyce Jonkman and Teresa Crumpton, thank you for all your prayers and encouragement during the process of writing this book.

To my sisters in Christ, prayer warriors, friends that I can count on to intercede and pray for me. Julie Coy, Mary Bajareno, Joyce Jonkman, Juli Perkins, and Ana Acuna.

To Chavos, my sister in Christ, for praying for me, encouraging me, and proofreading this book when I first started writing it. Thank you to you and your husband, Garry, for wanting to publish this book. I appreciate all your hard work, vision, and gifts in getting this book published.

To Teresa Crumpton, my editor/coach who is also my sister in Christ and whom I call friend, thank you so much for all your hard work on this book. Thank you for the encouragement to keep writing and for everything you taught me about writing, editing, and God.

Contents

Introduction..1

1. New Journey to Freedom 3
2. True Body Image 9
3. Fearfully and Wonderfully Made 19
4. Biblical Women & Inner Beauty 25
5. Freedom to Enjoy Life..31
6. Behold the Bridegroom's Beauty.....................41
7. Created for His Good Pleasure........................45
8. Covered with His Beauty...................................49
9. A Season of Shame..55
10. Time for Change 65
11. The Beauty of Friendship 75
12. Fascinating Love..79
13. The Beautiful Shepherd....................................85

14. The Beauty of Motherhood 89
15. A Heart of Worship 99
16. Giving Thanks to God 103
17. God Won't Let Us Down 107
18. Come to a Quiet Place 111
19. The Beauty of Journaling 115
20. Tea with Little Ole Me 119
21. The Lessons of a Garden 123
22. Go to the Countryside 129
    Notes 133
    About the Author 135

Introduction

My story is every woman's journey toward self-acceptance and the understanding of true beauty. I was embarking on a new journey of freedom, love, and enjoying life. I had discovered the King with new eyes that captured all of His beauty. I experienced an endurance and strength found only through His grace and was able to accomplish new goals and dreams He had set before me. He gave me the strength not to give up—no matter what obstacle or struggles I encountered.

The King showed me that I possessed an inner beauty I didn't even know I had, and He revealed to me what true beauty really was. These seasons with my Bridegroom helped me become confident of who I was to Him, and eventually I was able to see these things in myself. I started believing what He saw in me, and I felt like I could accomplish anything with Him on my side. These truths led me to this new journey, which began in a new year. My precious time in the garden spent face-to-face with my Bridegroom the King was coming to an end. It had been a beautiful season. The garden had been a place of comfort and security for me. I felt safe and confident there, but it was time for those truths to be put to the test.

I knew very well the peer pressures I'd face: dictates from society's false paradigms that women have to look a certain way, weigh a certain weight, or even dress in a false fashion just to fit in. It's a trap, a façade—because outward beauty is fleeting. The King revealed to me how women possess an inner beauty that is only found through His Son Jesus, the Bridegroom, the real paradigm of true beauty and perfect love. My journey is your journey. (My journey with God—to understand inner beauty—took place over a five-year span and continues.) Keep reading to discover the revelation I had of true beauty created by God and what I learned from my successes, failures, and disappointments.

New Journey to Freedom

Winter

It was a cold winter morning in Missouri. I was sitting in an overstuffed floral chair, my usual area where I'd write and sometimes journal. The sunroom was painted ocean breeze blue to remind me of the ocean waves from California where I grew up. I'd spent my summers at the beach getting suntanned. Oh, how I missed the ocean, but here in Kansas City I created a space for myself that was so peaceful. I would light up candles on the coffee table and put on an instrumental music CD to enhance the mood.

I held the new journal in my lap and ran my fingers over the embroidered pink rose cover. I smiled, opened the first page, and began to write. "What do You have to teach me this year, Lord?"

Inner Beauty

January 1

It's a new year, new goals, new visions, new hopes, new dreams, new destinations to explore, and a brand-new journey. I am feeling so much joy and excitement for the new year. God, let me be completely devoted to You, for I am hidden in You. Guard my heart from other lovers. I choose to put on the shield of faith.

I am able to edify others. You have made me fruitful. It is time to nurture others. You say I am pure, innocent like a dove, covered by Your glory. You chose me.

And as I was writing, Philippians 4:13 kept coming to my mind: "I can do all things through Christ who strengthens me."

Every new year I write a list of goals—New Year's resolutions, all attainable, but some take longer. Some of last year's goals I gave up on due to circumstances beyond my control, but others I gave up on because of discouragement.

"I know this year is a different journey. It's not going to be the same. With God's help, I won't give up again." I heard a faint whisper.

"You can do all things through Christ who strengthens you."

I began declaring over myself, "I can do all these things by Your grace. Your grace is sufficient for me."

Then He said to me, "My grace is sufficient for you, for my power is made perfect in weakness."[1]

Yes, Lord, Your grace is sufficient for me.

One of my goals was to get healthier, lose weight, and increase my physical strength. So, one morning in January before heading to the gym, I prayed: "God, I need help and accountability in this area."

I walked into the gym, and as I was scanning my membership card, Jamie, the gym owner on the other side of desk, noticed me and asked, "Are you getting the most out of our gym?" Her smile was warm and sincere.

I was surprised at how much Jamie genuinely cared for my well-being. But I felt embarrassed because I had not given it my all. I had been so busy that past year. I said, "I would if I were consistent and changed my eating habits."

Jamie had no way of knowing about my prayer that morning, but she challenged me to master the Curves diet and volunteered to keep me accountable.

"I hate the word *diet*. I can't eat anything I like," I said.

"I know you can do it, Bella." Jamie put away some of the members' files.

"I'm not even so concerned about how I look. It's how I feel. I feel so self-conscious and tired all of the time."

"Think how nice it will be to have your strength back." Jamie sounded excited. "You'll have energy to do anything you want."

"I want to regain my strength, be lighter on my feet, have the energy to do things, and be able to wear heels again." I laughed. I so longed to wear dresses again, to feel feminine and pretty in pink. I loved the color fuchsia. "I bought a fuchsia dress and new heels that I have not been able to wear."

"Overall though, health is a great motivation," Jamie said.

I felt challenged, and I knew what I needed to do. I said, "OK, thanks for your help. I'm going to need it."

Inner Beauty

After wrestling with the idea for a few weeks, I decided to commit to starting the diet and counting on Jamie for accountability. I began strength training three days a week and taking thirty-minute walks three to four times a week. I also decided to keep a journal to write down the calories of everything I ate. This was a totally new challenge because up until then I'd only kept journals of my everyday experiences and spiritual journey—not calorie counting. Just the thought of it irked me.

"God, I don't know if I can do this. Really, I don't want to do this, but if this is going to help me then, please give me the grace to do this."

Little did I know this was going to turn into a longer journey than I thought, one with twists and turns, a roller coaster with ups and downs and major stops. When God does a work in you, it's not quick; it's a process because He's more interested in healing the inward than fixing the outward. He's more concerned about developing our characters than solving our problems.

Prayer...

God, show me those areas You are calling me to believe with You that I can do in Your strength. Give me the grace to do them, and let me see what You see, the journey that You have for me. I choose to trust You and rely on Your strength and Your power to do all that You are calling me to do.

Reflection...

1. What is God challenging you to do that maybe you feel like you can't do in your own strength? Name the areas.

2. Do you tend to rely on your own strength or on God's strength?

Challenge...

Ask a friend or sister in Christ to pray with you, encourage you, and keep you accountable. Consider all the things you are tempted to do alone instead of relying on God to give you the strength.

Remember you can do all things through His strength. He is for you!

True Body Image

A Rainy February Day

I opened the window a crack to listen to the rain and to smell the fresh air. I unfolded a blue quilt, wrapped it around myself, and snuggled in the overstuffed chair. On those gloomy days I loved sitting in front of the window to journal. I let out a big sigh, grabbed my journal, and began to write. "God, I am not doing well. I am really struggling with this diet and losing weight." I was not even expecting God to answer. I just wanted to vent on paper.

All of a sudden God brought memories of when I was in grade school and the lies I believed about myself:

- I was an ugly duckling because I didn't look like the skinny supermodels on TV and in magazines.

Inner Beauty

- I had to be rail thin just to be considered pretty.

I remembered all the years I was discontent with my body shape, my weight, and my facial features. I was never happy with the way I looked. I became obsessed staring at the models on the glossy magazine pages.

And when I was in high school, I looked in the mirror and was convinced that I was fat, even though I really wasn't overweight at that time. I compared myself with the anorexic-looking airbrushed models. It made me feel unattractive, and I thought I would never have a boyfriend. I hated shopping for clothes because I felt nothing looked good on me. Back then I sat for hours in front of the mirror putting on makeup and trying different hairstyles. I so longed to dress and look like the models in the magazines. But the more I compared myself with these models, the more I hated myself.

For years I tried the latest diet or weight-loss program only to lose the weight and gain it all back again. Frustrated, I began skipping meals, but then it progressed to starving myself to then overeating. I hated to look in the mirror and shop for clothes. I struggled with vanity and low self-esteem.

Later on, as a young adult, I started getting attention because my looks had changed for the better. It now had become vanity, and my focus was on myself. My outward beauty became my worth, my identity. Later, as an older adult, my body changed, and I gained weight. My metabolism slowed down, and I blamed disappointing circumstances in my life. I ran to food instead of God. Food had become my comfort instead finding comfort in God.

I went through seasons of depression. Years of the same cycle: losing the weight to losing the victory and regaining the weight. This went on for many years until I allowed God to bring truth and healing to my heart.

I learned that it wasn't a weight issue; it was a heart issue, an identity crisis. All these years my motivation wasn't for health reasons but for appearance, vanity. I believed the lie that if I looked good on the outside, I would feel better about myself on the inside.

When my pen fell to the floor, I snapped back to the present in the snuggly chair by the window, and this question kept coming to my mind; I knew it was from God.

"What are your motives for losing weight?"

I knew the answer to this question, and God knew the answer to this question, but He wanted me to hear the truth out loud.

"It's for appearance." I could barely get the words out.

"Your motives should be about being healthy and taking care of your body, the temple I gave you so that you are able to do the work I have set before you to do."

"I know, Lord. You're right; give me the grace to continue this weight-loss journey for health reasons."

This was a total shift from years past. God wanted me to go deeper into those issues of my heart and the inner core of my being—how I felt about myself and the old lies that would attack my mind. God was reminding me of my value and that beauty was not based on my outward appearance. Somewhere along my journey I had fallen right back into that false body image because of all the weight I had gained back and failing again and again.

I thought about all the young girls and women that struggle with this same issue.

"How many women and young girls also believe the lie that they are ugly? How many are bound by outward appearance? How many battle with weight issues, struggle with eating disorders, starve themselves, skip meals, or overeat?

"How many believe this lie that we should put our value in outward appearance rather than in the truth of what God says about us and how He sees us?"

The Statistics of Women and Their Bodies

One evening I picked up a health magazine and flipped the pages. I came to an article on body image. I wasn't surprised when I read the following statistics:

- Four out of five women in the US are unhappy with their appearance.[2]
- Only 11 percent of girls globally are comfortable using the word *beautiful* to describe themselves.[3]
- A study showed that women experience an average of thirteen negative thoughts about their bodies each day, while 97 percent of women admit to having at least one "I hate my body" moment each day.[4]
- Eighty percent of women agree that every woman has something about her that is beautiful, but do not see their own beauty.[5]
- Seven out of ten women felt angrier and more depressed following the viewing of fashion model images.[6]
- Eighty-six percent of eating disorders present themselves before the age of twenty.[7] It's estimated that 11 percent of high school students are struggling with diagnosed eating disorders.[8]

Is it fashion? Is it media pressuring girls to think that if they don't like their body image, they can just have plastic

True Body Image

surgery? I continued reading and found these statistics on plastic surgery.

Cosmetic surgery has been one of the biggest boom industries of the twenty-first century, and it has also been abused. People become addicted to looking perfect for vanity reasons.

Over half of all teens (52 percent) feel that the media pressures them to change their body image, and 73 percent of teens feel their appearance affects their body image.[9]

The statistics were astonishing to me, and I felt overwhelmed and compassion for all these women and young girls struggling with these same issues.

The wind had changed direction and was blowing rain in the open window. A crack of lightning caused me to jump.

I cranked the window closed and saw my faint reflection in the glass. I redirected my thoughts to this question: "So why did I buy into this false body image when true beauty comes from inside?"

I continued staring at my faint image in the glass and remembered all too well those years before I understood what true inner beauty was. I stopped writing and thought about my friend Vosann. I put down my journal and picked up the cup of hot tea. The wind was still blowing, and I watched the tree branches moving back and forth.

"Poor Vosann had to go through so much to learn what true beauty was."

Inner Beauty

Vosann's Story

Like me, Vosann had compared herself to other women and the models in the magazines.

"Oh, look at their flawless skin. I wish my skin was like that," she said.

She not only struggled with acne-prone skin but with a false body image too. God made her with a slender frame, and others made fun of Vosann because of it. They called her "Olive Oyl" and "Skinny Minnie." Their cruel words would replay in her mind and heart. Over and over, they reminded her, made her believe the lie: "You are ugly."

This hit at her sense of worth, and she took on a false body and beauty image. She didn't see herself rightly through the eyes of God but with eyes of comparison. She began to seek God in prayer to see herself as He saw her. He did just that.

She had an encounter. She felt Jesus's presence. She felt Him hugging her and telling her how much He loved her. He loved and accepted her no matter what she looked like because in His eyes, she was beautiful. She began to see herself rightly. From that one encounter with Jesus, Vosann was never the same again. She started declaring what God had spoken to her heart, based on Psalm 139:14.

> I am beautiful. I am fearfully and wonderfully made!

True Body Image

In her pursuit of realizing this beauty, she still wanted perfect skin. She decided to get a skin treatment, and her face ended up getting severely burned. The welts left ugly scabs. This tragedy became the final breaking point in her process to true beauty and freedom.

Now the shame she felt over the scabs was ten times worse than her acne, and no amount of makeup could cover the scabs. She received lots of encouragement from family and friends during this devastating time. This helped her endure to the end of the journey to true beauty.

The enemy intended this incident for evil, to totally destroy her. Yet God used this tragedy to totally deliver Vosann from a false body image, the perfect skin syndrome, and low self-esteem. Through this process she realized what true beauty was and how beautiful God had created her. It wasn't about her outward appearance and having the perfect skin but about her heart. God started healing her skin. Her skin started becoming clear and beautiful. What the enemy intended for evil, God turned around for good. He declared His goodness over Vosann.

Vosann's story is one of many testimonies that God truly wants to set women free of this issue. He wants us to celebrate and accept the body He gave us.

Prayer...

God, thank You for revealing to me that I am fearfully and wonderfully made, that I don't have to compare myself to a false image that fashion magazines or Hollywood portrays, because You created us all unique. Give me the grace to continue this weight-loss journey for health reasons and not outward appearance. Help me not compare myself to other women. Give me the grace to meditate on Your Word, which will encourage me and build my self-esteem and confidence in the person You created me to be.

Challenge...Ways to Celebrate Your Body

1. Celebrate the body God gave you.
2. Set goals to achieve physical and emotional health, rather than obsess about your physical appearance.
3. Participate in a physical activity you enjoy doing. This will not only improve your physical health, but it will also boost your self-esteem and help you feel better.
4. Dress in a way that makes you feel good right now; do not focus on what you can wear once you lose weight.
5. Look in the mirror without judging yourself and making negative comments about your body. Rather declare Psalm 139:13-16:

    For you created my inmost being; You knit me together in my mother's womb. I praise You because I am fearfully and wonderfully made. I know that full well. My frame was not hidden from You when I was made in the secret place. When I was woven together in the depths of the earth, Your eyes saw my unformed body.

True Body Image

All the days ordained for me were written in your book before one of them came to be."

Inner Beauty

Crying Girl

This girl has cried more than the rain,
Yet, she smiles every day just to hide away the pain...
She tries to stay strong, but every day she feels weak,
Tired of wiping away each tear that rolls down her cheek...
No one knows her story; no one hears her heart.
I think she wanted to die, right from the very start.
She imagines her future, in a world that seems bleak.
She can't find the answers in the truth that she seeks.
She's hanging on tight, although she doesn't know what for...
Her heart is screaming for someone to hear,
down to her core...
She's forcing a smile...with all the strength that she has left.
There's only ONE who's different and isn't like the rest.
God is holding her for she can no longer stand—He kisses
her pain; her tears fall into his hand.
He whispers, "I'll never leave you, though everyone has.
I won't hurt you like every single person from your past..."
She sighed a deep breath, because she almost gave up...
But God came in time, and filled her empty cup...
With love, peace, and only a joy he could give—He gave her
hope, and a reason to live.

—Khiarra Vasquez

Fearfully and Wonderfully Made

For lo, the winter is past, the rain is over and gone.
The flowers appear on the earth...
Song of Solomon 2:11–12

It was spring, and I was looking forward to enjoying my garden again. I went outside and collected my blue watering can and headed for the flower garden. I was greeted by the singing birds and an amazing display of white irises, pink and yellow tulips, and violet trumpets and lilies.

"How beautifully designed these flowers are. As beautiful as I have designed you," whispered God.

As I plucked some daisies to put in a vase, I thought how beautifully God had designed these flowers—each one different in shape, color, and fragrance.

The seasons when certain flowers grow differed too. Some could withstand freezing temperatures, while others were fragile. Some grew with more heat, some with less. Some flowers had beautiful fragrances like the roses in my garden. Each flower was uniquely created with a special meaning such as the daisy, which means innocence and hope. Just like flowers differ, women do too; we have different body shapes and features, but we are all beautiful.

We all carry a beautiful unique fragrance, and we are a sweet aroma to God.

> For we are a sweet aroma of Christ to God, in those who are saved, and in those who perish.
> 2 Corinthians 2:15, NHEB

We are all beautiful women because God created us. God's Word states that we are fearfully and wonderfully made (Ps. 139:14).

> You are altogether beautiful, my love; there is no flaw in you.
> Song of Solomon 4:7, ESV

God's Word should be the final authority on what true beauty is, not Hollywood or a fashion magazine.

Since this is obviously majorly important in our lives, I've devoted a whole section to it.

I knew what it was like to wrestle with the truth of what God said about me and how God viewed me versus how I felt and viewed myself. As I walked through the flower garden to pick out some more flowers for my flower arrangement, this phrase and question kept coming to my mind: "Beauty is in the eye of the beholder." And who is our Beholder? I knew this was not from scripture, but God wanted to show me that man looks at the outward to judge. Man is always observing and giving his opinion about what is beautiful. God judges by the heart and not the outside.

> For the LORD does not see as man sees; for man looks at the outward appearance, but the LORD looks at the heart.
>
> 1 Samuel 16:7a

If God accepts who we are and what we look like, then why don't we? He is the one who created us. Why wouldn't He accept the ones He created? We were created in His image, and God is beautiful. Therefore, we reflect the beauty of God.

After I picked a basketful of flowers, I sat on my garden bench. I heard God say to read Genesis 2.

> And the Lord God formed man of the dust of the ground, and breathed into his nostrils the breath of life; and man became a living being....And the Lord God said, "It is not good that man should be alone; I will make him a helper comparable to him."...And the Lord God caused a deep sleep to fall on Adam, and he slept; and He took one of his ribs, and closed up the flesh in its place. Then the rib which the Lord God had taken from man He made into a woman, and He brought her to the man. And Adam said: "This is now bone of my bones and flesh of my flesh; she shall be called Woman, Because she was taken out of Man."
>
> Genesis 2:7, 18, 21–23

"Incredible," I thought. I had read this many times before, but I never really thought of this beautiful God, the Creator of the universe, creating woman out of a man's rib. An awesome wonder, God created us as majestic creatures. We are created to reflect God's beauty, His image. I fingered the purple iris growing nearby and pondered this thought.

My body is made of billions of cells. All my organs function together. This can only be explained by a loving, majestic God—the Creator and Designer of the universe. God numbered my very hairs (Luke 12:7). I kept repeating: "Our hairs are numbered. Every human being on this earth—each hair is numbered!"

As I sat there still in awe, the sparrows in the birdbath caught my attention, and I heard a gentle whisper from God: "See these little sparrows; I care for them. I feed them, but are you not more valuable and more precious than they are?"[10]

I smiled as I watched two sparrows splashing in the water. "You look exactly the way I intended for you to look. Fearfully and wonderfully made. Unique."

But God wanted to reveal more to me. God wanted me to become confident of who I was and my true identity. God wanted me to have the right perspective of my body image and to believe that I was fearfully and wonderfully made. And more than outward beauty, attaining goals and accomplishments, God wanted me to grasp this very truth about *inner beauty*.

Prayer...

Thank You, God, for revealing to me what true inner beauty is. When I see magazines or TV models, help me remember not to compare myself to them. Outward beauty is fleeting, but a heart that loves and fears You is worth more than outward beauty.

Reflection...

1. Do you struggle believing that you were fearfully and wonderfully made by God?
2. Do you tend to compare yourself to other women or girls? Why?

Let's see what true inner beauty looks like with these women in the Bible.

Biblical Women & Inner Beauty

I got up from the bench to walk around the garden, and God brought to my mind a few women in the Bible. Everything alive portrays a reverence for God, including the inner beauty and strength we—as women—possess.

Deborah the Patriotic Military Advisor (Judg. 4:4-10)

Deborah was both a prophetess and a judge (Judg. 4:4). As a prophetess, God used her to deliver His messages to His people. As a judge, God gave her the authority to settle disputes as well as enforce the law.

Ruth, the Woman of Constancy

Ruth was faithful and dependable in serving her mother-in-law. Ruth was known for her true love and selfless giving. She left her father and mother to live among unknown people. She wanted to serve her mother-in-law. She found favor in God's eyes and with Boaz, a man of wealth. Ruth was also known as a woman of strength.

Hannah, Wife of Elkanah

Hannah was barren, distressed of soul, and praying to the Lord to give her a child. Later, she was blessed with a child and dedicated him to God. She was a woman of prayer and never gave up until God answered her prayer (1 Samuel 1–2).

The Warm-hearted Shunammite Woman

The Shunammite woman was hospitable and had a kind heart, a contented spirit, and a persistent nature. She took in Elisha, a man of God, gave him food and prepared a small upper room for him to sleep in. Then, when her son died, Elisha prayed for her son, and God answered his prayer for the Shunammite (2 Kings 4:8–38).

Huldah, a Prophetess

Huldah was a powerful spokeswoman for the Word of God. She revealed God's message to national leaders and unveiled the future of a nation. Huldah's standing and reputation are attested to in that she was consulted. She could be found sitting in the central part of the city ready to receive and counsel any who wished to inquire of Jehovah. (See 2 Kings 22:14–20; 2 Chronicles 34:22–28).

Queen Esther

Queen Esther, whose Hebrew name was Hadassah, had neither father nor mother, but was raised and adopted by Mordecai, her cousin. She was very beautiful and obtained favor in the sight of all who saw her. She found favor from the king, who made her his queen. God then used her to risk her life to save her people, the Jews (Esther 1–9).

Out of all of these, one woman stood out to me the most, and that was Esther.

She and the virgins had to go through beauty treatments for a year just to look beautiful for the king, as if Esther wasn't already beautiful enough. But according to the laws of Persia this is what they had to go through before they could be presented to the king.

I sat back down on the bench in my garden and picked up my Bible and turned to the story of Esther. I had read it before, but it had been a while, and I began to read Esther 1–2.

It was in the year of 483 BC when King Xerxes ruled over 127 provinces, and reigned from his royal throne in the citadel of Susa, and in the third year of his reign he gave his banquet for all his nobles and officials. King Xerxes commanded Queen Vashti to be brought to him, but she would not. So, it was decreed that Queen Vashti was never again to enter the presence of King Xerxes. In other words, she was exiled, and now King Xerxes was advised to look for another

Queen. In those day's what Queen Vashti had done was wrong not only against the King but also against the nobles and the peoples of all the provinces of King Xerxes. Then King Xerxes' personal attendants proposed that a search be made for beautiful young virgins

The selected virgins were required to eat the finest foods, rich foods and not foods that made you thin. The young women had to be well nourished because in those days, thinness was a sign of poverty. I thought how that was interesting because in today's society thinness is in. How times have changed. A paradigm shift.

Aren't we women blessed to know that we don't have to go through beauty treatments to go before our King—the one true King, Jesus, who declares over us that we are already beautiful, that beauty is really something we already are and not something we do to look beautiful?

But what else made Esther stand out? It wasn't just her outward beauty and the fact that she was chosen to be the next queen. It was something she did.

Esther fulfilled a greater purpose than just becoming a beautiful queen for an earthly king. Esther had a destiny, though she went through having to sacrifice her own plans, was an orphan, leaving behind the only family she had—her cousin Mordecai. Yet Esther's destiny was fulfilled and had nothing to do with the plans she had in mind for herself. She was destined for a greater purpose—to save her people, the Jews. We are all destined for greatness.

> For I know the plans I have for you, declares the LORD, plans for welfare and not for evil, to give you a future and a hope.
>
> Jeremiah 29:11, ESV

Esther was judged by her outward beauty. But later she was recognized for her courage, her inner strength, her *inner beauty*.

God says you have stolen my heart with one glance of your eyes. He is ravished by our beauty. He says, be encouraged that God sees a beauty in us that is not external.

How beautiful you are, my darling! Oh, how beautiful!
> Song of Solomon 4:1, NIV

Esther stood up for her people; she was courageous even though afraid. She possessed an inner strength and courage she probably didn't even know she had. Esther had to overcome herself to do what God had created and positioned her to do.

Esther faced the fear of being killed going before the king and standing up for her people. More than just beauty, she became a woman of valor. I don't think we are born with bravery, but we definitely can be put in situations where we can choose to be courageous to fulfill the God-given calling on our life.

Esther overcame her desire for self-preservation to fulfill what God wanted her to overcome. All these women in the Bible showed a reverence for God. They all had a prayer life. They were all favored by God. Some were in leadership and authority roles. Some were spokeswomen. Some gave of their time and resources. Some had great faith and strength. Some were wives and mothers.

All these women portrayed an inner beauty that is pleasing to God. And whether you're a wife or not, Proverbs 31:10–31 is a great example of what true beauty is. I was so inspired and convicted that I prayed to God that morning:

"God, more than fulfilling my dreams, my plans, and what I think is my destiny, I'd rather fulfill a God-given destiny to be a blessing to others and not myself, to bring to death my agenda for a greater destiny and purpose being fulfilled that has nothing to do with me.

"You are more concerned about my character than my outward beauty and accomplishments. Give me the grace, boldness, and courage to be obedient to the assignment You have given me to do on this earth."

Reflection...

1. What woman in the Bible do you relate to the most and why?

2. What woman in the Bible do you wish you were more like? What characteristics does she have that you would like to have?

3. What are some things that God might be pointing out to you or is already working on your heart about?

God is faithful to complete the work He has begun in you.

> And I am certain that God, who began the good work within you, will continue his work until it is finally finished on the day when Christ Jesus returns.
> Philippians 1:6, NLT

Freedom to Enjoy Life

It was spring, and I was outside in my garden enjoying the yellow daylilies. Everything was blooming earlier because of a mild winter. This was a treat for me because I loved to be outdoors sitting on my white, wooden bench with intricate carving where I would journal and meditate. That particular morning, I felt compelled to write a list of goals and dreams I had for the coming year, but even after writing those goals and dreams, I thought: "My goals, dreams, and visions have to have a bigger purpose than just goals and dreams being fulfilled. I want them to be inspired by God. I want to have a bigger purpose and to make a difference in someone else's life. It's not about making myself known, but about making *God* known."

Inner Beauty

I didn't realize at the time that this was going to be more than just attaining the many goals I had in mind.

God started showing me another side of Himself I had not yet experienced. I started seeing Him in a different way, which expressed more of His character. He was bringing out qualities and creativity in me I never knew I had. He started giving me new desires. He gave me the idea to turn all my journals into a book that would encourage women.

He also gave me the desire to take a photography class to capture His beauty through landscape photography. I even had the idea to create a magazine in the future featuring short stories and nature photography. I wanted to turn my poems into songs. It was like I was coming alive and dreaming again.

Although this was more than I could believe for, He revealed to me that if He was in me, then I carry His glory. I carry His light, His creativity, His love, and I was made in His image. He was revealing to me that He is so much more than just what I had known about Him. He's an artist who expresses His artistry. He is our teacher who teaches us all things through the Holy Spirit. He is the healer who heals our hearts and emotions. He is the painter who paints our lives into a beautiful tapestry. He is the potter who creates and molds us into the image of Christ. He's the musician who writes and sings songs over us. He's a melody who catches our ear if we listen. His whole presence is beauty, love, passion, justice, righteousness, purity, and holiness.

There are so many facets of God that are unending. He is the true Bridegroom lover of our souls, the defender for justice and righteousness, the lover who captivates hearts for himself, the author who writes our story, the beginning and the end. He's the father to the orphan, and the husband to the widow and divorcee. He's the friend to the friendless, and

Freedom to Enjoy Life

He becomes our everything when we have nothing.

I closed my journal and went to bed that night thinking of all that God was revealing to me. I felt overwhelmed with joy and awe. It didn't stop there, though. It caused a desire for me to learn more about who God is. I looked forward to going out into my garden every day to hear from God so that He could reveal more to me.

God was challenging me in so many different ways. Turning all my life experiences into a story was just an idea, but now with the revelation that God was showing me, it was becoming a reality in my life. Throughout that year, God kept showing me that I possessed everything I was asking and praying for. I had everything I needed and everything I wanted to be because He lived in me. He reinforced through His Word that "I can do all things through Christ who strengthens me," including what I have set my heart and mind to do.

Whatever had bound me before, no longer had a hold on me. I experienced such freedom. I knew God was in all of my goals because those things that concerned me concerned Him. I was now free to see God in all of who He was.

He started revealing to me that He isn't just in the four walls of a church building; He is into everything and is omnipresent. He speaks to us through His creation, and that in itself reflects His very nature.

For the first time I felt free to express my creativity in the arts through writing, photography, and music. I realized that fear of failure had always kept me bound from trying new things. There were opportunities to use my gift in singing, but because of my fear of failure or because I didn't think it was spiritual enough, I didn't pursue that gift and later realized with much regret I wished I had.

This new year God was setting me free to explore more

of what He wanted for me. He showed me I had more gifts inside of me than just singing. He showed me I had a gift in writing. I would wake up eager to write in my journal, and I couldn't stop writing all that God was revealing to me. I was filling page after page.

Sometimes we only see those things that are visible, but God sees those things we can't see in ourselves—those gifts, those desires, those dreams, and those visions that have been hidden deep in our hearts. Maybe those desires and dreams have become dormant because circumstances in our lives have caused those dreams and desires to die.

God wants to give us new dreams, new desires, and new visions. God had given me new eyes to see with, a new heart to love again with an increased depth, a new faith and hope to believe for what is greater, new dreams to dream the impossible, new breath to breathe, and a new life to live again. He breathes new life in our hearts to live for Him, to believe, to hope and have faith in Him again.

I was now living, dreaming, and enjoying life again. I was enjoying my new friendship with Penny, who I met at a Curves, and those around me. I was losing weight and gaining strength and energy to do those things I couldn't do before—like hiking and walking. I was going to gardens and hiking trails I have never been to; I was doing things I never even thought I would enjoy, but I came to love. I saw God's nature in the gardens and nature trails.

It was like I was seeing God with new eyes. I wanted to capture all His beauty through photography. I was remembering how much I'd loved photography when I was in high school. I had also enjoyed writing stories and poetry in English class. It was in high school where I developed a love for journaling.

Freedom to Enjoy Life

Somewhere along the way I had forgotten that I loved doing these things. These things had brought life and joy to me, but I had gotten distracted with the years that were full of pain, trials, disappointments, and just plain life. God brought back those desires from long ago for me to pursue now.

God wanted me to enjoy everything around me: the people in my life and the earth that He created for us to enjoy.

We are all a reflection of God's beauty.

When I fully came to the revelation that He lived in me, that He enjoyed me, and that He loved it when I would spend time with Him, it was a delight to my heart. It was where I felt the most joy.

> As for the saints who are on the earth, They are the excellent ones in whom is all my delight.
> Psalm 16:3

I pondered this thought: "He delights in us; we are excellent because He is in us, Christ the excellent one, the hope of glory. His promise to us is that He will show us the path of life. For He is "the way, the truth, and the life" (John 14:6).

> In your presence is fullness of joy; At your right hand are pleasures forevermore.
> Psalm 16:11

> For whatever finds me finds life, and obtains favor from the Lord.
> Proverbs 8:35

And I did. I found life in Him and life more abundantly. Every day that I would spend time with God and my Bridegroom, Jesus, He gave me hope for the future, grace in the trials, and joy instead of sadness. I enjoyed life in Him, which caused me to enjoy those around me and everything in my life. I didn't want to just exist and survive life; I wanted to thrive, to make a difference in people's lives, to be a history maker, and to impact the world. I wanted to proclaim God's beauty and joy through the arts throughout all the nations. I sensed God speaking into my spirit: "My people are bound from pursuing those dreams and visions I have put inside of them. They are kept from pursuing them because of religion, unbelief, and the cares of this world. I have put dreams and visions inside of you to further My kingdom, but unbelief has stolen those dreams.

"Those visions have become distorted somehow from the cares of the world. I'm setting My people free, free to soar, free to fly. I am giving you the grace not to give up, the grace to fulfill all that I have purposed in your hearts to do by My grace. And my grace is sufficient for you. You were created to do great exploits for Me."

Jesus said, "Very truly I tell you, whoever believes in me will do the works I have been doing, and they will do even greater things than these, because I am going to the Father" (John 14:12, NIV).

I was feeling so overwhelmed with joy, I stopped writing and closed my journal and ended with this prayer.

Prayer...

Thank You, God, for creating me to enjoy life and life more abundantly. Show me how to do that and bring You glory. Empower me to do the greater works You created for me to do on this earth. Bring life to those dreams and visions that You have put in my heart to pursue. For apart from You I can do nothing, but with You I can do all things because You strengthen me and give me wind for my wings to fly.

Reflection...

1. What are some dreams, goals, and visions God has given you that have become dormant?

2. What do you think are some reasons that have kept you from pursuing these dreams or accomplishing these goals?

3. Are you ready to pick them up again and believe God for the greater purpose of those dreams, visions, and goals?

I stand with you to believe again, dream again, soar, fly high, and find the freedom to enjoy the abundant life God created for us to enjoy.

Inner Beauty

Luz's Story

Like me, other women struggle in this area of losing our identity in the workplace. Let me tell you about my sister-in-Christ and friend Luz, who had worked for the same company for more than thirty years—a job that she'd enjoyed. Then Luz got laid off, and it was unexpected. She felt worthless, like a loser. She felt so many emotions, like depression, fear, insecurity, and a lot of anger for being laid off. She felt lost, confused, and as if she were paralyzed. She was stressed and worried. Luz had always been independent and had always taken care of herself, and now she was having to depend on God to provide.

In that season of not working she spent more time in prayer and had more time to meditate on God's Word, which renewed her mind. God revealed to her that her identity was not in her job and what she did, but her true identity was in who she was to God. Her value was not in her job, because she was already valued by God. Luz was blessed to have a husband who prayed for her and encouraged her. She also had sisters in Christ and a pastor holding her up in prayer.

Luz began to heal from the loss of her job. God gave her two scriptures to believe and stand on.

> It is God who arms me with strength and keeps my way secure.
>
> Psalm 18:32, NIV

So he said to me, "This is the word of the LORD to Zerubbabel: 'Not by might nor by power, but by my Spirit,' says the LORD Almighty.

Zechariah 4:6, NIV

When Luz started to feel worried, she also declared this over herself: "All my worry and anxiety that tries to steal my peace, health, and sleep each night are rendered powerless, because I know now that God is my only source physically, mentally, emotionally, and financially."

He showed her that if she called upon Him, He would answer:

He will call on me, and I will answer him; I will be with him in trouble, I will deliver him and honor him. With long life I will satisfy him and show him my salvation.

Psalm 91:15–16, NIV

He showed Luz that it was His strength she needed to rely on, and not her own. He showed her that she was not alone, and that He was with her. God also revealed to her how much she was loved by Him. He wanted her to experience His infinite love that nothing and no one in this world can give. God's love is pure. She was falling more in love with Jesus and feeling the Father's love.

Like myself and many women, Luz also struggled with a false image of herself. She didn't know how beautiful she was to God. He revealed to her how beautiful she was and that she was perfect and flawless. He revealed to her that she had been made in the image of God and that she was fearfully and wonderfully made.

In that season of not working she learned so many things. She experienced much healing and came to know who she truly was, but God wanted to bless her even more. God wanted her to enjoy life to the fullest. She felt free, free as a bird. He gave her the freedom to travel. He showed her that she didn't have to wait till retirement, but she could enjoy life now. God provided financially and the opportunity for her to travel with her husband. Luz was able to do so many things she couldn't do when she was working.

Luz was available to care for her family and her mom, and help her brother with his court cases. She can look back and say that God had better plans for her, more than she would have thought for herself.

Sometimes we can't see what God has for us in the future, where we are going to be needed. We may feel worthless and useless, but God doesn't waste time. He shows us what a loving father He is and how much He loves us. He shows us He's our provider, our healer, our defender and our first love. He shows us how much He wants to bless us, heal us, and restore us. It reminds me of those seasons of not working and how God used that time to teach me, heal me, restore my health, and give me so much more than a job or anything on this earth could ever give me.

He calls me to come to Him and spend time with Him, because He wants me to taste and see how good He is.

> Come, all you who are thirsty, come to the waters; and you who have no money, come, buy and eat! Come, buy wine and milk without money and without cost. Why spend money on what is not bread, and your labor on what does not satisfy? Listen, listen to me, and eat what is good, and you will delight in the richest of fare.
>
> Isaiah 55:1-2, NIV

Behold the Bridegroom's Beauty

Late Summer

I was home, outside in my garden, and the lawn was lush green. Trees were fully budded, and the summer flowers I had planted were in full bloom.

The gladiolus, lilies of the valley, pansies, and violets brought beauty and fragrance to my garden. I walked around the water fountain and was reminiscing of the time spent in my garden journaling, enjoying the different seasons of weather and the different seasons in my life. I was thinking about all the inner healing that God had brought into my life. The years of learning more about God and His Son, Jesus, the Savior of the world, but also a Bridegroom who loved his bride—me.

Inner Beauty

I thought of the mentors God had brought into my life to help me along my journey and the countless hours of beholding His beauty in the garden.

I sat on my bench and wanted to write in my journal all that was in my heart: "What an excitement to serve God, loving Him and allowing Him to love me. I was created to be loved, and I have seen God's handiwork in all that I have accomplished in this last year, but I know that no goal, no dream, no accomplishment could ever compare to beholding the radiance of the Lord.

"I no longer want to have an outward beauty that is fleeting, but I desire an inward loveliness that can only come from the Son of God, Son of Man."

Though Jesus was described (in Isaiah) as having no outward beauty, He beheld an inward grace in me that is only received through accepting Him and knowing Him. It could not be bought; but it was given as a free gift. He is chief among ten thousand. There is only One who represents true *inner beauty*, and it is not defined by outward appearance. Only when we accept Him can we see and Him.

> One thing I have desired of the LORD, that will I seek: That I may dwell in the house of the Lord, all the days of my life, to behold the beauty of the LORD, and to inquire in his temple.
>
> Psalm 27:4

Let the beauty of the Lord our God be upon us. He beholds a beauty of holiness. He is a royal diadem, who gives us beauty for ashes. For those areas in our inward being that are dark, broken, and wounded, He restores and provides inner healing. He is perfect, yet He desires to perfect those areas in our hearts, in our inner being that are not yet perfect. He is the one who makes everything beautiful in its time. He has also set eternity in the human heart.

> ...To comfort all who mourn, to console those who mourn in Zion, to give them beauty for ashes, the oil of joy, for mourning, the garment of praise for the spirit of heaviness; that they may be called trees of righteousness, the planting of the LORD, that He may be glorified.
>
> Isaiah 61:2–3

I had so cherished those prior seasons of beholding the King's beauty, sitting in His garden, being ravished by His love. I wouldn't trade those seasons for anyone or anything this world could offer. To behold the beauty of this King is more precious than gold.

> You are fairer than the sons of men; grace is poured upon Your lips; therefore God has blessed You forever. Gird Your sword upon Your thigh, O Mighty One, With Your glory and Your majesty.
>
> Psalm 45:2–3

Jesus is most beautiful. Most valiant, a valiant warrior, who will fight for justice, who will fight on your behalf. He is the most excellent of all men, who stands for righteousness and justice. He is the King of kings and Lord of lords, and He rules. The government is on His shoulders. He is majestic. He is ravishing beauty. He is adorned with sapphires, beautiful majestic gems.

He is clothed with righteousness and splendor—a magnificence no one can fathom. He is glorious. He is dazzling, eternal God. And He loves His bride like no other. He captivates hearts like no other.

Who can compare to His glory? What can compare to His Love? He is the One who causes hearts to ache for Him, the Rose of Sharon, the true beholder of beauty, majesty and glory. Selah (pause, and think of that)

Prayer...

God, open our spiritual eyes to behold the beauty of Your Son, Jesus. He is the one who heals hearts and loves us like no other. He is more beautiful than any woman or man on this earth. He is King, He is the Bridegroom, He is a friend, and He desires for us to behold His beauty because He is worthy.

Created for His Good Pleasure

Fall

Fall was coming to an end, and I was enjoying what could be my last days outside before winter came around again. I was sitting outside on my garden bench, savoring the sun's rays because I knew these days wouldn't last long. Most of the garden had spent its blooms, but I smiled at the patches of chrysanthemums, still happily flowering. "They'll stay until the first hard frost," I thought. Chrysanthemums and pumpkins are my favorite, and I wanted to enjoy them as long as I could. As I gazed over the garden, I sensed God impressing something on my heart about humankind.

I picked up my pen and began to write: "God wants humankind to know Him, but man has separated himself so far from God. It's like they think they existed on their own. They worship creation and themselves more than they worship God the Creator. Many have wandered from the faith or backslidden to follow the gods of this world: money, fame, perversion, or prestige. There is only one true giver of life, only One who can satisfy. "How can we know the Creator of the universe if we don't spend time with Him, if we don't commune with Him?" I wondered. How can we love Him if we don't even know or believe He first loved us and He sent His Son, Jesus, to reconcile us to Him, Father God?

From the beginning God created a garden, a paradise for Adam and Eve, a place to enjoy, a place to commune with God, to fellowship with Him. I put down my pen and picked a yellow chrysanthemum. I spun the flower between my hands, staring at the many perfectly formed petals. God has given us something even better; He has given us an eternal place with Him, a garden locked up in our hearts.

Jesus Christ is our Beloved, our Bridegroom, and we can experience paradise now. It's not a place. It is a state of being. It's our relationship with Him. Because we have distanced ourselves from Him, He was sent as a ransom for us, a demonstration of God's love for us. How can we not accept the one who created us and the One who sent his Son to reconcile us with himself?

> All this is from God, who reconciled us to himself through Christ and gave us the ministry of reconciliation
>
> 2 Corinthians 5:18, NIV

Song of Solomon describes a lush garden full of orchards of pomegranates and pleasant fruits; spices of fragrant henna, spikenard, saffron, clams, and cinnamon; and trees of frankincense, myrrh, and aloes. It was a fountain of gardens, a well of living waters and streams.

He says to us,

> You are a garden locked up, my sister, and my bride;
> you are a spring enclosed, a sealed fountain.
>
> Song of Solomon 4:12, NIV

What a beautiful place to commune with God, Abba Father, our maker. We have this place to look forward to in the heavenly realms. Yet, we can experience a garden, a paradise, in our hearts with Him now and share it with others. A tear trickled down my cheek.

"Oh, how I long to share it with a world that only sees darkness, a world that has no hope. They don't even know they were created to experience such a love, an unconditional love with their Father, Abba Father God." I looked at the flower again and thought that they could have their own love story with their Bridegroom, Jesus, Son of God; one day He will return for a bride who has been captivated and drawn by His love. There is no greater pleasure, no greater intimacy, no greater love than knowing my God and my Bridegroom.

Prayer...

God, use me to make You known to a lost and dark world, to make known Your love to those that don't know You. Perfect me in Your love so that others will see Your unconditional

Inner Beauty

love and be drawn to You. Open our eyes and heart to see that we were created for Your pleasure and goodness so that You can enjoy us and we can enjoy You. Your Word says that "You created my inmost being; You knit me together in my mother's womb. Your eyes saw my unformed body and all the days ordained for me were written in Your book before one of them came to be" (Psalm 139:13,16 NIV).

Let our hearts' cry be that we want to know You, to see You, and to hear Your voice. We are Your beautiful creation and goodness.

Covered with His Beauty

A Beautiful Snowfall

The holidays came and went, and now we were in January. I was anticipating this snowfall that the weather station had predicted was coming, but I was not expecting it to be this beautiful.

I woke up to a gorgeous snowfall. I grabbed my thick robe off the chair and ran to the window. Everything was covered in white—branches, trees, bushes—just breathtaking! "God, you really do make everything beautiful!"

> [God] does great things which we cannot comprehend. For He says to the snow, 'Fall on the earth'; likewise to the gentle rain and the heavy rain of His strength.
>
> Job 37:5–6

Inner Beauty

I had woken up extra early so I could see this beautiful spread. Everything was majestic white; big flakes had fallen, the ones that stick to the branches and trees like God's fingerprints. I couldn't wait to go outside and take pictures, but I was still tired so I went back to sleep for another couple of hours.

When I finally woke up, I ran quickly to the closet, put on my jacket, and went to the garage door that opened to the yard. I looked outside and breathed in the fresh cold air. I was in awe of this magnificent snowfall.

My husband, James, got up too and looked out the window. "Wow, it's so beautiful," he said. "I can't wait to go out there, but first I'll make some breakfast."

James made his usual breakfast, hash browns and fried eggs; after he was finished he called me. "Bella, breakfast is ready."

I came in and hurriedly ate my breakfast because I couldn't wait to go back outside to take pictures.

I put on two layers of clothes, snow boots, hat, and gloves. James was ready to go too. We weren't able to drive anywhere because our driveway and the streets were covered with snow and not yet plowed. So, we had to enjoy the snow in our backyard, and we had plenty of snow to enjoy—about two acres.

Naturally, I tried to capture all this beauty with my camera. I hoped I could capture some really good pictures. James and I were enjoying the outdoors and taking many pictures of ourselves and our dog Ringo in the snow. Then James said he'd better start plowing that snow out of the driveway. I remained in the backyard, where I got an idea to put some birdseed on top of the birdhouse, since it had a pile of snow on it. I hoped that the male cardinal would land there. To my amazement after maybe ten minutes of waiting, I saw a vibrant red cardinal land on a snow-covered branch.

I thought, "Oh, my gosh, God help me to take a good picture of this."

I didn't have time to run in the house to get a tripod, so it was now or never.

I positioned my camera to take a picture; my hands were shaking. I whispered, "God help me to keep my hands from shaking, so I can get a few shots of this cardinal."

And gosh darn it. I did. "I got some!" I yelled. "Thank You, thank You, thank You."

I felt like it was a kiss from God. I was able to take a number of pictures of this stunning red cardinal. Whether the photos looked professional or not (I didn't know much about photography), I was ecstatic just to get some shots of the cardinal.

What a day after a beautiful snowfall, breathtaking, and with a bright red cardinal right on a snow-covered branch. It really was a gift from God!

After this exciting moment, I felt so curious to get on the internet and search information on cardinals.

I read that "cardinals are songbirds, and the male uses its call to attract a mate. Unlike most northern songbirds, the female also sings."[11]

I felt blessed that I got to enjoy these singing cardinals in my garden all the time. I kept reading: "Females will often sing from the nest, a call to her mate. Cardinal pairs have song phrases that they share. If you listen carefully, on the first sunny days of late winter, you may hear the cardinals' song. It sounds like 'cheer, cheer, cheer' or a short 'chirp.' During courtship, the male feeds the female seeds.

"This is so interesting," I thought, "because it's like a bridegroom courting his bride. It is also a reflection of Jesus when He courts His bride."

He feeds her continuously with His Word, and His love, and he claims, "This is My beloved, My sister, My bride. Daily He feeds her with words of love and encouragement, and He tells her how beautiful and lovely she is.

I was feeling so loved by God and remembering my seasons in the garden with Jesus. "What a beautiful demonstration of a bridegroom and bride-to-be." Just like this male cardinal feeding his future bride in the garden, and declaring his territory, this beautiful Bridegroom Jesus was declaring, "This is My bride, My beloved, she is Mine, and I am so captivated by her beauty. I so want to cover her with My beauty, the beauty of My love."

I clearly remembered a season experiencing this kind of love, wishing I could go back to that season, when I had been kissed by the Bridegroom, but I knew I was on a new journey, a new season. God wanted to take me even deeper, and with that comes new experiences and new revelation. I was feeling so grateful, and I thanked God for continuing to reveal His love.

Prayer...

Thank You, God, for the seasons of love and intimacy You want all of us to experience.

Show us and draw us to those seasons of love and deeper intimacy with You.

Show us what that looks like individually, because You created us all unique, and You know what moves our hearts.

Cover us with the beauty of Your love, and captivate our hearts to want to seek You in the secret place.

Reflection...

1. What are some ways Jesus has shown You His love?

2. What season in your life has been the most rewarding where you have experienced the love of Jesus?

3. Is there anything holding you back from experiencing His love—trust, past wounds, unbelief? If so, ask God to show you what that is and surrender it to Him and allow Him to bring healing to your heart so that you can go deeper in your relationship with Jesus.

A Season of Shame

A year had passed, and I had been busy that summer with work, writing, working out, and planning a summer vacation, which included a family reunion. Everything was going great that summer, but after getting home from my trip, there were disappointments awaiting me.

A job fell through that I was so looking forward to. The editor I was working with was not going to meet my deadline for my book to get done that I had so hoped for. The reality was my book still needed a lot of work, and worst of all, my family relationships were broken.

Soon my workouts stopped, the holidays were right around the corner, and I gave in to every treat and eating out that I thought would bring me comfort. I felt confident that I could lose the weight again, but eight months had passed. I got very busy at work, and no exercise and eating unhealthy foods took a toll on my health, weight, and energy.

I didn't dare weigh myself because I knew I had gained some weight back, but I did not want to know how much weight. I could not fit into last year's summer clothes. I was feeling so defeated. I thought to myself: "It wasn't enough that I had regained some weight two winters ago and was able to get it off by the summer, but again?" I couldn't believe I went through another winter, stopped working out, and ate all those Christmas goodies.

I hadn't just regained a few pounds, but all the weight I had lost plus ten more pounds. How could I have gotten myself to this place again? The shame of going back to the gym was unbearable—having to face the owner and my teammates, who'd looked up to me and rooted for me when I had lost all that weight. I felt like such a failure. The shame kept me from going out in public—my clothes didn't fit and I didn't feel physically well.

The shame of eating out in public and the thoughts that people might be thinking bothered me. "Does she really need to be eating?" I felt like I was being watched. It was an endless torment going through my head. And how could my husband be attracted to me when I had gained so much weight? It was really tormenting me. It was damaging my relationship with him because I felt so insecure. Though he reassured me he loved me no matter the weight gain, it still affected me in every area of my life. It affected me spiritually, physically, and emotionally.

A Season of Shame

And this wasn't the first time. It had been years of this same cycle of losing and regaining—an endless battle and asking God what the root cause was.

And God spoke so loudly in my spirit that it sobered me up: "Disappointments."

I had to repeat it to myself, "Disappointments!"

It spoke volumes to me, and I knew exactly what He was getting at. I knew the disappointments very well.

Disappointments from other people, false expectations, being let down, and letting others and myself down.

I knew I wasn't the only one that struggled with this issue. I tried to remember not to focus on my outward appearance again, but how could I not when my stomach was bulging out of my pants. Thinking I could fit into the same size, I had bought new summer clothes, and I could not fit into to them. Was I in denial? I knew I had gone up a size, but I dare not go back into the store and return the clothes.

"I am not going to buy bigger clothes! I am going to lose this weight!" I blurted.

Past motivation and what I had done in the past wasn't helping. My husband, James, had more confidence in me and would tell me, "You did it once before, you can do it again."

Was this going to be enough to motivate me once again? The shame, the regret of giving in to the love of food, the false comfort it brought, the guilt—this was a lot to face. And it wasn't just the guilt. It was now the conviction of overeating and not taking care of my body.

Inner Beauty

Being overweight really kept me from feeling physically fit, emotionally sound, and spiritually strong. It kept my focus on myself rather than on others and the things God wanted me to focus on. I judged myself by my outward appearance. How could I have fallen into this trap again? I let the beauty of that precious year just slip through my hands.

I knew too well the bondage, the shame, and all those things that it kept me from pursuing—those things God was calling me to do.

God was showing me that I was running to the false comfort of food because of the disappointments that had occurred in my life.

This was a battle I'd been fighting for many years. I would gain victory and would fall right back into that place of overeating and gaining the weight again. I knew that God wanted to set me free from this bondage—the shame, being overweight, and unhealthy eating. God wanted me to be whole in every area, to prosper in every area—my spirit, soul, and body. God wanted me to be completely whole and healthy. There are issues or things in my life that were hindering me from being completely whole. And I thought, "How will I make it work this time permanently?"

I knew I would face disappointments. I mean this is just part of life.

And I heard God say so gently, "One day at a time; don't look to tomorrow or days ahead—just one day at a time. Make good decisions today and every day that you face. With the truth of My Word, make war against the lies and temptation."

I prayed, "What will I do differently? God help me to love You more, more than food, more than the false comfort food brings. Give me wisdom to choose healthier foods for my body; give me grace to exercise and stay active and the wisdom to know when to rest. Give me the self-control to not give in to those treats and the grace to eat in moderation and not eat those foods that are harmful to my body."

Through this time, I also learned all the foods I was allergic to that were not good for my health. These were foods that I really enjoyed. Although it was going to be hard, I knew that God would give me the strength to avoid them.

I knew I had to declare war against this battle of overeating and eating those foods that caused an allergic reaction. I knew there were going to be downfalls, but the important thing was to get back on my feet and keep believing, keep declaring the truth that I can do all things through Christ who strengthens me. But more than just doing the right things and declaring truth over myself, God wanted to take me deeper to the core of my inner being, to the shame that still kept me in bondage. The shame of failure and still feeling unworthy.

One morning while I was doing my Bible study, I came across this topic: "Do you see what he sees? Seeing our worth." By the end of the chapter I was weeping from the inner core of my being. Have you ever wept so deep that you knew God was doing a deep work in your soul? God was exposing the lies that I was still believing that I wasn't worthy of being healthy and having a healthy body.

He revealed to me that I was worthy of being healthy. I was worthy of knowing the right perspective of my body image. I was worthy of walking in divine health—body, mind, soul, and spirit.

"If you see that you are worthy, you will take care of the temple I gave you. You will see yourself as I see you. You are a precious gem. You are worthy to be loved. You are worthy of the abundant life I want to give you. You are worthy to be happy and full of joy. You are worthy of My healing. You are worthy of My goodness and My blessings."

The scales started falling off me. I believed what God was showing me. I felt so free and full of joy. I was overwhelmed by God's presence and love.

I made a promise to myself that whenever I started feeling unworthy, I would declare these truths over myself:

- "This temple that You gave me is worthy of being taken care of."
- "I am worthy of being healthy."
- "I am worthy of being healed."
- "I am worthy to live the abundant life."
- "I am worthy of having a healthy body, mind, soul, and spirit."
- "I am worthy of God's love."
- "I am worthy of God's goodness."
- "I am worthy to be happy and full of joy."
- "I declare life and life more abundantly over myself."
- "Your blessings will overtake me, and You will do more than I can ask or imagine."
- "I am worthy!"

A Season of Shame

Challenge...

I challenge you to declare this every day for thirty days. It takes thirty days to change a habit, so instead of speaking negative things about yourself, speak this and see the changes take place. I am with you!

Inner Beauty

Julie Coy's Story

Like myself, Julie also had her seasons of shame. In her late thirties Julie started breaking out with psoriasis on her whole body, due to a lot of stress in her life. Problems in her marriage and struggling with depression took their toll. Julie felt ugly and ashamed of her body. She believed the lies that she was unworthy, unlovable, and ugly. Julie would cry a lot.

She didn't want her husband to look at her, let alone touch her. Julie had suffered with this disease for fifteen years along with diabetes. She lived with this shame for years until she started drawing closer to God, and He revealed truth to her.

Julie knew she needed to make some changes, but she also knew that she couldn't do it without God's strength. She went to church and women's Bible studies, which is where she was encouraged by other women. She learned to cry out to God and give Him her worries. She spent more time meditating with worship music and reading the Bible to bring truth and healing to her mind, soul, and heart. She learned to not let her emotions consume her. Her bathroom became her prayer room. She would look in the mirror and declare what God spoke over her.

"I am beautiful! This disease and stress will not consume me, and I do not listen to the lies about myself."

As Julie spent more time with God, she learned who she was in Christ—that she was worthy and beautiful. He spoke to her that she was beautiful inside and out, and her value was not based on outward beauty, but inward. She learned not to believe the lies that the enemy whispered in her ear. She learned not to even entertain the lies of the enemy, but to take every thought captive and bring it to the obedience of Christ.

> We demolish arguments and every pretension that sets itself up against the knowledge of God, and we take captive every thought to make it obedient to Christ.
>
> 2 Corinthians 10:5, NIV

Julie would look in the mirror and start declaring over herself: "I am beautiful beyond description."

> I can do all things through Christ who strengthens me.
>
> Philppians 4:13

And when she started feeling depressed or sad she would quote:

> The joy of the Lord is my strength!
>
> Nehemiah 8:10b, paraphrased

Julie not only learned to take care of her spirit, but also her health. She learned that certain foods caused the psoriasis to flare up, so she would stay away from them. She started taking walks and eating healthier.

As Julie was taking care of her spirit and her health, she started seeing more healing in every area of her life: her heart, her emotions, her spirit, and her health in physical body. The psoriasis started fading, and Julie became confident of who she was, who God said she was.

Inner Beauty

Julie continues to seek God and to give Him praise for what He has done her life, her heart, her soul, and her health. She can say in confidence that God has been with her through the storms, and He has declared to her that she is unsinkable.

She is a woman of God, a woman of prayer and praise, and she gives God all the glory.

10

Time for Change

One morning I was sitting in one of the back rooms of the house that I named the lighthouse room because of its decorated lighthouse pictures and painted sea breeze colored walls. On occasion, I like to sit in this room and go read through my old journals. I picked up one of the journals, and it was pretty current from a few months ago, and I had written that if I wanted change, then I needed to do something differently. It read in big letters: IF YOU WANT DIFFERENT RESULTS THEN STOP DOING THE SAME THING.

Obviously if I keep doing the same thing, and it's not working any more, then it's time for change. If I want to lose weight, then my diet needs to change. If I want to feel

Inner Beauty

physically well, then I must do whatever it takes to help me feel better. If I want a better job or something I enjoy doing, then I need to go back to school, take some classes and work toward the change that I want.

Sometimes fear of failure keeps us from taking those steps towards change. It's easier to stay in the same rut because it's a familiar place, and it feels secure. Change gives us the opportunity to step out in faith with God. He works in us and for us to see those changes come about because He is faithful to accomplish what we can't in our own strength.

I have a social media mentor I follow, and she is always doing or saying things I wish I had the courage to do or say. It's like she's reading my mind. We think so much alike. She's bold, and she is not afraid to speak her mind, and I love that about her.

She inspires me to change. She motivates me to want more of life and more of God. She motivates me to enjoy God, life, and those around me. To see the positive instead of the negative. To be thankful for what I do have and not focus on what I don't have.

Being thankful in all circumstances is key to enjoying life to its fullest. We all go through seasons of hardship that steal our joy and our peace, but God's promise to us is that we may have and enjoy life in abundance—to the full, till it overflows.

> A thief is only there to steal and kill and destroy. I came so they can have real and eternal life, more and better life than they ever dreamed of.
>
> John 10:10, MSG

Time for Change

God is always calling us to want more of Him. To spend time with Him. To talk to Him and to listen. To pray to Him. From my own experience when I spend more time in worship, prayer, and scripture, I desire more of Him. I can't get enough of Him, and it causes me to want more of Him. When my life has no time for God, and it is just filled with my everyday duties, work, the cares of this world, and things of the world that don't nourish my spirit, it makes my heart dull.

Another thing I admire about my mentor is that she encourages me not to give up on the things God has promised me, but to keep moving forward with His help and a lot of hard work. God is on my side, and He is for me, and I can trust Him! And you know what? God is on your side. God is for you too. You can trust Him. He loves you.

> God told them, "I've never quit loving you and never will. Expect love, love, and more love!"
> Jeremiah 31:3, MSG

God is always doing something new, and sometimes we can't see that new thing He is doing because we are stuck in the present circumstances or what's happened in the past. I really love this version of this scripture. It gives so much detail, and it gets right to the point.

> This is what God says, the God who builds a road right through the ocean, who carves a path through pounding waves, the God who summons horses and chariots and armies—they lie down and then can't get up; they're snuffed out like so many candles: "Forget about what's happened; don't keep going over old history. Be alert, be present, I'm about to do something brand-new. It's bursting out! Don't

you see it? There it is! I'm making a road through the desert, rivers in the badlands. Wild animals will say "Thank you!"—the coyotes and the buzzards—Because I provided water in the desert, rivers through the sun-baked earth, drinking water for the people I chose, the people I made especially for myself, a people custom-made to praise me.

Isaiah 43:16–21, MSG

I remember before we even thought about moving to Kansas City, Missouri, God started showing us it was time for change. We were not sure what that change looked like, but we knew in our spirits that change was coming. The process wasn't easy. We were going to leave all our family behind and move to a new state where we didn't know anyone.

We had to wait for God's timing and confirmation that this is what God was leading us to do. We were afraid and not knowing how this was going to happen, but we said yes to God, stepped out in faith, and God made a financial way for us to move.

The new job that opened for my husband paid for our moving costs. They typically didn't do that, but God gave my husband supernatural favor with the company. This company also agreed to my husband's asking salary amount and full medical insurance benefits. We knew then that this was God's will and plan for us, because He had given us these three things we had asked for and was making a way for us to move.

With God's help, we can move forward to the change He has in store for us. This year I sense change is coming again. He has been encouraging me to call out to Him, and has been assuring me that He will answer and show me the great things He has in store for us. He is faithful to answer, and He always provides when it looks impossible. God can do this for you too. I am not special in any way. He loves us all the same, and He has great things for all of us. It may not look like moving to another state. He has different plans for all of us, and they are good for us.

Prayer...

God, open my eyes to see the new thing You are doing. Give me a new mind-set and the faith to believe for the great and impossible things You are going to do in my life. Deliver me from old mind-sets that keep me from moving forward. Give me new faith to walk it out. Give me grace to trust You with the plans You have for me.

Reflection...

1. Is God calling you to have a new mind-set in a certain area or circumstance in your life?

2. Do you see God doing a new thing in your life? If not, ask God to show you the new thing He is doing in your life?

Inner Beauty

Challenge...

Ask God to show you what lies or old mind-sets are holding you back or keeping you from seeing the new thing God wants to do in your life.

Time for Change

Juli Perkins-Santorsola's Story

It was summer, and I was so grateful for the season I was in. I was able to workout again without any breathing issues and remembering how sick I was. I thought about many of my friends, who'd helped me along the way, and Juli was one of them. She had been praying for me and introduced me to cleansing and probiotic supplements. Juli was thriving with energy and health, and she was losing weight so much that it inspired and motivated me to continue working on my own health and weight loss, but Juli hadn't always been this way.

Juli—like myself—had believed the lie that she was overweight in junior high school, when in reality she was not. Juli also would look in the mirror and believe the lie that she was fat.

Juli also suffered from premenstrual depression disorder (PDD) and anxiety due to her hormones being out of balance. She also suffered with vertigo.

Juli—like myself—had contemplated suicide, but thank God for His intervention. Without Him, neither Juli nor I would be around to share our story. When Juli got married and started having kids, she also suffered with postpartum depression. The only time she wasn't depressed was when she was pregnant. She suffered with emotional eating, which led to gaining weight. Being overweight, feeling depressed, and having anxiety really took a toll on her emotionally and physically. Juli had suffered with this for more than twenty years, and all her doctor would do is prescribe her antidepressants, which were not healing her.

At the age of forty-four, Juli was tired of being overweight and still suffering with depression and anxiety. She knew she had to make some changes. She started taking walks and changed what she was eating. She successfully lost fifty pounds. The depression and anxiety lessened, but was not completely gone. Though Juli had lost a lot of weight, she was still not happy and was not healthy.

She started going to a women's Bible study that one of her friends had invited her to. She eventually went back to church, and that's when things really started to change for Juli.

She started to learn to lean on God for everything. She was so encouraged by her friend, and the pastor's wife, which is what she needed in that season.

Her faith in God helped her to run to Him instead of to food, which was a false comfort. Two of Juli's favorite scriptures encouraged her on this journey.

> Keep me as the as the apple of your eye; hide me in the shadow of your wings.
>
> Psalm 17:8, NIV

This scripture helped her when the enemy would attack her with anxiety. Juli learned to hold on to God's Word to sustain and encourage herself.

> If you say, "The LORD is my refuge," and you make the Most High your dwelling, no harm will overtake you, no disaster will come near your tent. For he will command his angels concerning you to guard you in

all your ways; they will lift you up in their hands, so that you will strike your foot against a stone.

Psalm 91:9–12, NIV

This scripture let her know that God was always going to be there for her and that an army of angels was protecting her.

God also started showing Juli about taking care of her body and health. He revealed to her that, like in Daniel in the Bible, she should eat natural foods instead of processed foods, which cause so much disease in our bodies. Not only did God want Juli to take care of her spiritual being, but also her physical body and gut health. Juli was introduced to a cleansing and probiotic supplement that helped get her get gut healthy.

These supplements she was taking also helped her break through a plateau, and she lost an additional twenty pounds. The depression and anxiety started decreasing even more.

Juli was thriving in the knowledge of getting gut healthy and taking better care of her body. She started feeling healthier and happier.

Juli learned so many things that she wanted to share these tips to encourage women.

- We as women need to take better care of ourselves first, so that we can take care of our families well.
- Do not look at yourself in a negative way because God made you perfect the way you are.
- As long as you are healthy—no matter your size or weight—health is more important.
- Find joy in the things that are right instead of what's wrong.

Inner Beauty

- Enjoy the small victories.
- Don't be hard on yourself.
- Find a program that works for you.
- Do not be obsessed with looking at the scale, but let the way your clothes fit and inches lost encourage you.
- Make small changes one day at a time.

The Beauty of Friendship

A friend loves at all times, and a brother is there for times of trouble.

Proverbs 17:17, ISV

It was the end of January, and February was right around the corner. January and February are the coldest months in Kansas City, Missouri, so I was looking forward to our trip to California and warmer weather. I was excited to visit with family and some friends I hadn't seen in more than five years since my dad's memorial service.

I was only going to stay three days, so I made sure I spent quality time with my mom. I wasn't sure how I was going to fit in my time with friends, but it worked out that the day before I was to leave two of my friends wanted to see me, and so we planned to meet at my mom's house. I was not planning the reconciliation that took place that night with my two friends, but I knew that God had ordained that day.

He wanted me to reconnect with them and forgive any prior offenses we had caused one another. But prior to this trip God had already been speaking to me and teaching me about friendship and how to be a good friend.

He was speaking about how to learn to forgive and to ask for forgiveness when we wound one another and to extend grace, because I needed just as much grace for my shortcomings.

God was teaching me that a friend loves at all times, and friends cover offenses and seek love. I was really being challenged in this area, and I had to decide whether I was going to choose to abide in God's love or continue staying in my offense and unforgiveness.

It's easier to stay offended than to forgive and to allow God to bring healing and restoration because that would mean laying down our rights and putting up walls of protection, so we don't get hurt again. God wants us to walk in love and freedom, and this is true for any relationship—not just friendships. He wants us to cover offenses with love, for love covers a multitude of sin.[12]

I am so thankful for all the friends God has brought into my life. I have friends that I can trust to pray for me and my family, and I do the same for them. I have also had friends that when we haven't spoken or seen each other in a while, we don't get offended. We just pick up where we left off.

I've learned that some friends come into your life for a season and others for a lifetime. I've also learned to let go of some friendships because they were toxic and hindering my walk with the Lord. Some friendships I have held on dear to because they were God-ordained friendships.

The Beauty of Friendship

In the case of one of my friends I hadn't seen in more than five years, God wanted to bring reconciliation, closure, and for me to let go. The other friend I was to reconnect with so that God could restore our relationship to a better and stronger relationship. God is always about restoring and reconciling relationships if we allow Him to, but it requires humility, work, and faith.

I've learned that the beauty of friendship can cause us to grow, to learn from one another, to love, to forgive, and to extend grace when we fall short. I've learned to hold on, to cherish, and to let go of friends when God said to let go. The beauty of friendships is that they are like the seasons of the earth. I've had the pleasure of experiencing the four seasons here in Missouri—winter, spring, summer, and fall.

Some friendships are like the winter season; they grow dormant and cold. Some are like the spring, the season of new beginnings with new friendships. Some are like the summers; they are the warmest and enjoyable season of the year. And some are like the autumn when leaves turn into beautiful foliage. A time of harvest and a time to gather— A season to give thanks for God's blessings.

No matter what season we are in, God remains the same yesterday and today and forever. He is faithful. I have also learned that Jesus sticks closer than a friend or brother. He is sometimes our only friend in those seasons I call the "winter" season.

> A man who has friends must himself be friendly, but there is a friend who sticks closer than a brother.
> Proverbs 18:24

Inner Beauty

Prayer...

God teach me how to be a friend. To love at all times. Teach me when to hold on and when to let go. To give grace and to forgive. But most of all to trust that You will always be there no matter what season I am in. That I can count on You to be the best friend I need.

Forgive me God when I have judged instead of extending mercy to those friends that have wounded and offended me. Let me extend the same grace You give me when I fall short of Your glory. Help me love unconditionally.

Reflection...

1. Are there friends in your life that you know without a doubt God put in your life?

2. Are there friends in your life that you need to forgive? Do you need to ask for the grace to let go of the pain and allow God to bring healing or reconciliation?

May God give you grace, my friend, to forgive and extend mercy over judgment. He is faithful.

Fascinating Love

It's Sunday afternoon, and I am sitting on my couch in awe of God's goodness. The night before, I had gone to a women's conference, and I was in amazement of how quickly God had answered my prayers from that morning. I had prayed that He would show me His love and that I would feel His love, because I felt like something was in the way of that, and I didn't know what it was.

That morning my heart's cry was that I just wanted Jesus to reveal Himself to me. I just wanted Him and nothing else. Nothing that this world could offer could satisfy this longing in my heart. I felt a sweet love, but it was not like years before. I felt my heart aching, and I felt the busyness of life take up all my time away from spending time with Jesus.

My Morning Prayer

This prayer was the cry of my heart that morning. "God, I want to be undone. I want to desire Your love and unquenchable fire. My desire is to know You deeper, Jesus. I want You more than money, more than the riches and pleasures of this world."

I kept repeating it over and over: "Jesus, I just want You! All I want is You! You're all my heart desires. I feel like I can't get enough of You. Your presence, Your love, this unquenchable love. A love I have never felt before."

God doesn't always answer me that quickly, but I believe it was His will for me that day. His heart's cry for me was to want Him more than anything. He was more concerned about my heart condition than answering all my prayers to fix the circumstances in my life. He wanted my surrender. I hadn't realized that there were areas in my life that I had not been willing to surrender to Him. I was scared even after I'd said the words, "God, I surrender." I mean, do I really have a choice? Well yes, I do have a choice, because He does give us a choice, a free will to choose His way or our way.

It was not just part of my life He wanted; He wanted *all* of my life. Full surrender would require total trust in Him and not knowing what He has in store for me.

I had forgotten that I was bought with a price. I had forgotten that my life was not my own anymore. I had forgotten that when I gave my life to Jesus, it was now His will for my life, His purpose in my life, and not my own.

In my years of being a Christian I had never seen someone so yielded to Jesus like Heidi Baker. She is the CEO of Iris Global, a Christian humanitarian organization, and is also an author of several books. Baker gave up her comfort-

Fascinating Love

able life in California to be a missionary in Mozambique, Africa. I know that we are not all called to be missionaries, but we are called to surrender our lives to Him and to be led by Him and to fully trust Him with our lives.

> Therefore I urge you, brethren, by the mercies of God, to present your bodies a living and holy sacrifice, acceptable to God, which is your spiritual service of worship.
> Romans 12:1, NASB

What does a life fully surrendered to God look like? I really believe Heidi Baker's life is just one example. She surrendered all to God and chose to live by the dump in the poorest city. She adopted all the orphans and became their mamma.

I know there are many more missionaries that have already gone to be with their Lord and many more in the present, but I mention her because she is one of my favorite ministers in the body of Christ. I was so moved by God's presence during the conference that it caused me to repent for not fully trusting and surrendering all my life to Jesus in serving him. I had my own plans, my own agenda of how I was going to live the rest of my life.

God was speaking very clearly to me that it was time for me to surrender my life to Him. I honestly had no clue. Here I thought I was doing the will of God with my writing and going to a 9–5 job and making plans to move to another state with our plans and agenda in mind. Our plan was to live a comfortable semiretired life and spend our weekends hiking and river rafting in the Colorado mountains and writing books about our adventures and God's beauty.

Inner Beauty

God was interrupting my plans by saying, "I am moving you, but not for the reasons you have in mind. I want you to serve in full-time ministry and go to the nations to proclaim My beauty and joy."

I questioned God. "How is this going to happen, and what is this going to look like?

I felt God speaking to me and saying, "I just want your yes, and leave the details to Me."

Honestly, I can say I have some history with God to be able to trust Him, after all He made a way for us to move to Kansas City; we said yes, and He provided a way.

Has God ever interrupted your plans? Well, it's very sobering. I call it His mercy in my life. If it wasn't for His love and mercy intervening in my life and messing up my plans, I would be heading in the wrong direction. Some of us are called to the marketplace to a 9–5 job, others to full-time ministry, but whatever we do, we all have a calling, and it's our responsibility to find out what it is. In His mercy and goodness, He shows us His plan, but in His wisdom, He doesn't always give us all the details about how it's going to take place. He knows when we are ready and mature enough to walk it out. He shows us when we are ready to surrender everything for the sake of serving Him, and because He is worthy, we say yes.

> ...we have not ceased to pray for you, asking that you may be filled with the knowledge of his will in all spiritual wisdom and understanding, so as to walk in a manner worthy of the Lord, fully pleasing to him: bearing fruit in every good work and increasing in the knowledge of God.
>
> Colossians 1:9–10, ESV

God speaks to all of us differently. We all have a unique relationship with God, and the way He shows me things may not be the way He will show you. We are all created uniquely, and He knows what moves our hearts and how to get our attention. He knows how to lead us, and He leads us well. We just have to be willing to listen. We have to be in a relationship with Him, and when we are straying from that friendship, He will send the alerts.

God doesn't just speak through our prayer time and reading His Word. He can speak in whichever manner He decides to use. I can be outside just enjoying my garden, and He will speak to me and show me things, or I can be at work, and He will put a thought in my mind and give me revelation about something to get my attention that will be confirmed through His Word. God is not limited in any way. He makes Himself known to us. He is not a respecter of persons.

Prayer...

God, help us to be alert when You are speaking to us. Give us a sensitivity to Your leading and when You're trying to get our attention. Give us the wisdom and understanding of all Your ways. God, show us our primary language in which You speak to us, whether it's through, dreams, visions, writing, worship, scripture, or prophecy, or small audible voice. God, give us ears to hear, eyes to see, and hearts to receive what You want to speak to us.

Inner Beauty

Reflection...

1. What are some ways God has gotten your attention or interrupted your plans?

2. What are some ways God has spoken to you?

Challenge...

Ask God to show you what His primary way He speaks to you, if you don't know.

The Beautiful Shepherd

The Lord is my shepherd, I lack nothing. He makes me lie down in green pastures, he leads me beside quiet waters, he refreshes my soul.

Psalms 23:1–3, NIV

My Shepherd

Thank you, God, that you are my Shepherd. You tend to my every need. On those days I am discouraged, You speak through my sisters in Christ to encourage me and lift me up. You give me hope through Your Word to not give up, but to keep having faith, because Your promises are yes and amen.

Therefore encourage one another and build each other up, just as in fact you are doing.

1 Thessalonians 5:11, NIV

You provide strength and energy when I am weak to get those things done that are priority.

> He gives strength to the weary and increases the power of the weak.
> Isaiah 40:29, NIV

The Lord Provided

You have always provided my daily bread for me and my family in those seasons of famine when my husband was laid off from work. Sometimes it's been through a church food pantry, unexpected money, or putting on someone's heart to bring us groceries. You have never left me nor forsaken me and my family. You have been my Shepherd, and in You all of my needs are provided. I lack no good thing because You are my Abba Father.

And this same God who takes care of me will supply all your needs from His glorious riches, which have been given to us in Christ Jesus (Phil. 4:19).

You Give Me Rest

In Your presence I find rest and peace. Spending time with You in worship and in Your Word, is like sitting with You in green pastures. You cause my mind, heart, and soul to rest in You. You will keep me in perfect peace when my mind is stayed on you and not on the problem.[13]

You restore my innermost being. You heal my emotions and quiet my soul. You refresh me with Your sweet presence. It was Your presence during the seasons of grieving for loved ones who were walking in darkness that brought healing to my soul with Your perfect love that cast out all fear. You quieted my soul with Your peace.

> Whoever dwells in the shelter of the Most High
> will rest in the shadow of the Almighty.
> Psalm 91:1, NIV

You Guide Me in the Right Paths

I feel revived to continue the path You have for me to walk in. You lead me as a good shepherd does. I can trust You because You are a good leader. Your plans for me have always been for my best. You know my past and my future. You, knowing my failures or successes, do not limit what You can do for my future.

You can see the things to come and lead me in a straight path, so that I am under Your protection. I have a history with You that has taught me to trust You. I chose to follow Your direction for my life, and I learned lessons when I didn't. You always have a better plan, a better path, and a better future for me to walk in.

Prayer...

May I grow deeper and deeper in love with You and come to a greater revelation that Your love for me is greater and deeper for me than I know. May I continue growing from faith to faith and glory to glory and to know You in a greater capacity as Jehovah Raah, the Lord my Shepherd. You are Jehovah Rapha, the Lord who restores my health and heal my wounds. You are Jehovah Jireh, the Lord who provides all my needs according to Your riches in glory. You are Jehovah Shalom, the Lord who gives peace in the midst of test and trials. You are Jehovah Nissi, the Lord who is a banner of love over me. You are Jehovah Tsidkenu, the Lord who is our righteous Savior and clothes us with a robe of righteousness. And You are Jehovah Shammah, the Lord who is always there for me.

You are the great I Am, the Alpha and Omega, the Beginning and the End. Selah

The Beauty of Motherhood

> Rejoice always, pray without ceasing, in everything give thanks; for this is the will of God in Christ Jesus for you.
>
> 1 Thessalonians 5:16-18

I remember one morning I was in the living room crying out and praying to God regarding my daughter. I was asking for God to show her He loved her and how He views her.

I had asked several of my closest sisters in Christ to join with me to pray for her, and one of the responses I got from one of my sisters was to praise out loud. My spirit confirmed yes, I need to praise God and worship.

I started to worship and felt led to declare the song "Reckless Love" by Corey Asbury.

I stood in the gap for my daughter as if my daughter was

singing this song herself. I declared that there was no darkness, no mountain, no lie, and no wall that would restrain Jesus from surrounding her with His love. After about an hour of worshipping and praying, God started replaying my past—how broken I was, how I was living in sin, how I had no fear of God, and how I had so many misconceptions about Him.

I was reminded of my own sin, shortcomings, and failures as young adult and as a young mother. What I did as a young adult not only affected me, but my daughter and family members close to me. I had asked forgiveness before, and I knew God had forgiven me, but I think I needed a reminder of where I came from and how God had rescued me, delivered me, healed me, and restored me.

He came to me with arms wide open of unconditional love that led me to repentance. I had peace for the remainder of the day, but still my heart was restless that evening.

The following morning, I sat in my usual place in the living room where I spend time with God, pray, and journal. I asked God, "God, what do You have to say about my daughter and this situation we are facing right now?"

This was God's response: "I am calling you to a fast and intercession. There is still much more for you to learn about motherhood. Motherhood doesn't always look pretty; it is messy, dirty, and downright painful. No one said motherhood wasn't going to be painful. It doesn't feel good, doesn't look good, and there will be seasons of heartbreak.

"But that's where I, the great I Am come along. You need to cry out and stand in the gap for your daughter through intercession so that she will come to a revelation of the Father's love I have for her. When a mother's love or father's love falls short, I have a perfect love that heals, restores, and redeems.

The Beauty of Motherhood

I have a perfect love that casts out all fear and torment.

"I entrusted this child to you. Abide in Me, because in your own strength you can do nothing, but in My strength, you can do all things."

He also said that we as mothers were never meant to take God's place in our children's lives. No matter what decisions they make, no matter who they choose to love—it was not up to us.

We would like to have a say-so, especially when we see them heading in the wrong direction or about to make a big mistake. I'm learning that I don't always know what's best for my young adult daughter. I'm learning I don't always have a solution to her problems. But God does; He really knows what's best for our children even if it means going through heartaches, making bad decisions, and learning the hard way.

Our role as parents to our young adult children is to direct them to God—to fear Him and to love Him and to go to Him first before anyone else when they are facing challenges. I am learning our job as a mother is to love them unconditionally like God does.

It's not our job to change them, but to be an example and point them to God and His infallible Word. It is never our job to judge them, criticize, or beat them with the Bible, or theology; our only job is to direct their hearts to Jesus.

I know as parents we have fallen short of this and made a lot of mistakes, but there is grace and forgiveness in God.

God is so much bigger, and His love is so much deeper, purer, and unconditional. His love conquers all, but He can understand a mother's heart for her children. I believe He gave us that heart to want to nurture and protect our children from all harm. We're like lionesses when it comes to our children, but God loves our children even more than we do, and He wants to be their protector and their everything when we fall short. His answers to our prayers don't always look like we think they should. His ways and thoughts are so much higher, wider, and deeper. He sees the overall picture of what is yet to take place.

Sometimes He takes us deeper through pain, disappointments, and unexpected circumstance. But He is always faithful, and He always answers. He is the perfect Father and gives perfect love. I'm learning to have a heart like His. To love like He does.

I miss those times when my daughter was small, and I used to sing to her and teach her how to read. Those were priceless memories.

The adolescent years were the hardest, but they drew me closer to the Father for wisdom, strength, and more of His love.

The young-adult years are about learning how to let go and trust God. I think it's the hardest phase.

You learn that by helping them too much you're enabling them and making them to depend on you instead of depending on God. You learn that even your advice isn't always the best advice for their problem, because we think we know what's best for them.

You learn to ask if you can share your advice, rather than just give it. Sometimes we just need to listen and let them figure it out for themselves and trust that God will show them the right direction or solution. And then watch, pray, and be there when they make mistakes, because they will learn through their mistakes.

God is that way with us as His children. He always points us in the right direction, but sometimes we don't always make that right choice, and we learn, and He gives us grace to walk it out and get it right the next time.

It makes me think of Jesus's mother to have to see her Son go through excruciating pain to fulfill God's will for the world. I can't even imagine having to go through that, but I know He understands a mother's heart for her children.

> But we proved to be gentle among you, as a nursing mother tenderly cares for her own children.
> 1 Thessalonians 2:7, NASB

Prayer...

Thank You, God, that Your loving-kindness leads me to repentance when I need to repent and turn to You. Teach us how to have Your heart toward our children. You created them, and You know their hearts, and You know what moves them. Help us to get out of Your way and trust You when our children are wayward and heading in the wrong direction. I choose to trust You that You know what's best. You will give me wisdom in every decision and the grace and strength to walk it out.

Reflection...

1. Do you have children, nieces, nephews, or even a friend's child/adult children that you tend to worry a lot about because they are clearly with bad company?

Inner Beauty

Are they doing drugs, in jail, or heading in the wrong direction without God in their life?

2. Can you choose to trust God and surrender them into God's hands right now?

3. Are you willing to sacrifice time to fast and pray when God calls you to?

Hope's Story

A Mother's Intercession

I wanted to share my own mother's journey of intercession. Through Mom's thirty years of praying and interceding for me and our family, I have no doubt she has learned some things. But until I was sixteen years old, prayer and intercession was something my mom was challenged to put into practice. God had already been drawing my mom to Himself, but she'd not yet surrendered. When I was sixteen, I attempted suicide; I was a very depressed, broken, and wounded teenager. My mom had no idea about what I was struggling with. I mostly kept to myself.

It's a miracle that I am here to write about it, but it's what caused my mom to surrender her life to Jesus and to learn about prayer and intercession as a mother.

My mother started going to a women's Bible study and then eventually to church, having been invited by one of her friends. This is where she learned to pray, but not just to pray, to intercede—"to act or interpose on behalf of someone in difficulty or trouble, as by pleading or petition."[15]

My mom did just that. She stood on behalf of me and my family that we would come to know God. Well, God answered her prayers two years later because I got saved when I was eighteen. My immediate family members came later. God has answered so many prayers in her thirty years of praying.

My mom wished she had kept a journal of all the answered prayers. Some she is still waiting on, but here are several of the answered prayers.

Salvations in Our Family

My dad was one of the longest to wait on, but now he is in the presence of God.

My mom's life was spared through a car accident, the last thing she remembered yelling out was "Jesus." It's a miracle she is still here.

My mother was healed physically from all the pain and ailments in her body after the accident.

My mom prayed for sick people in the hospital, and they got healed. One night she prayed for a young man who was in a lot of pain. He was waiting to be seen by a doctor, but while waiting, my mom asked him if she could pray for him, and he said, "Yes, please." After she was done praying, he felt no more pain, and the young man was in awe. After that my mom shared about God's love for him.

God's Supernatural Provision

Once, my mom needed money for property taxes, and she prayed that the winds would blow money from the east, west, south, and north. Well, a few days later she went outside in her front yard to rake leaves, and she found five hundred dollars—just the right amount to pay her property taxes.

Family Members Delivered From Drug Addiction

They are completely set free now. One of the scriptures my mom would constantly pray for our family members was this:

Shall the prey be taken from the mighty, or the captives of the righteous be delivered? But, thus says the Lord; even the captives of the mighty shall be taken away, and the prey of the terrible be delivered; for I will contend with him who contends with you, and I will save your children.
>
> Isaiah 49:24–25

God answered a lot of prayers, but some she is still waiting on. She has learned that prayers don't happen in her time frame or even her way. She has learned that her ways are not God's ways.

> For my thoughts are not your thoughts, neither are your ways my ways, declares the LORD. As the heavens are higher than the earth, so are my ways higher than your ways and my thoughts than your thoughts.
>
> Isaiah 55:8–9, NIV

My mom also learned that she needed to pray using God's Word, because it's His will be done and not her will.

> So shall my word be that goes forth from my mouth; it shall not return unto me void, but it shall accomplish that what I please, and it shall prosper *in the thing* for which I sent it.
>
> Isaiah 55:11

She learned to wait on God's timing. Hearing testimonies through Christian television or radio is what has sustained her to keep believing, keep standing and not give up. Hearing those testimonies encouraged her and gave her hope.

In waiting for those prayers to be answered for her loved ones, God revealed to her that the person that she was pray-

Inner Beauty

ing for was not ready, but He is always working behind the scenes. Though she can't see things change or even the person change, God is still working, and he remains faithful.

> Not one of all the Lord's good promises to Israel failed; every one was fulfilled.
>
> Joshua 21:45, NIV

A Heart of Worship

It was Thursday evening, and I was home resting from a long day at work. I had been messaging my niece to encourage her with her new walk with the Lord. I wanted to send her some encouraging songs to listen to and told her that God would not let her down, and she can depend on Him to see her through the circumstances she was facing.

This song sung by Bethel Worship was about God never letting us down. As I was listening to this worship song, even though I was not expecting for it to be ministering to me, I felt God's loving presence and rest. I realized then I needed to be ministered to by God.

He reassured me that He would not let me down in my own circumstances. I felt His presence so strong that tears were coming down like a waterfall. I felt such rest that I let out a sigh of relief.

As I continued soaking in God's presence while listening to the worship song, I felt like my spirit had been so thirsty and longing for God's loving presence. God was satisfying my need that evening. He was speaking to my heart that He was bringing me back to a heart of worship. I had a longing to worship Him again, something I hadn't felt in a long time. I was too buried in my own wounded heart and busy life to even feel anything anymore.

I had felt so numb for years. God kept showing me in His Word that He was going to restore my relationship with Him. He kept leading me to Jeremiah 33:3. The whole chapter is about the promise of restoration.

> Call to me, and I will answer you and tell you great and unsearchable things you do not know.
>
> Jeremiah 33:3, NIV

God was showing me that when I call to Him He was going to answer me and show me great things. He was going to bring healing and show me His loving-kindness. He is a good God. I was already seeing this in my relationships with some of my family members. He was restoring my relationship with my brother, which I had so longed for, but more than my relationships with my family, I longed for my relationship with God to be restored.

He spoke to my heart: "I am bringing you to Myself. To worship Me. To trust Me. To long for Me again. Not to just worship Me in song, but to worship Me in spirit and in truth, My truth. Be a worship unto Me."

A Heart of Worship

Yet a time is coming and has now come when the true worshipers will worship the Father in the Spirit and in truth, for they are the kind of worshipers the Father seeks. God is spirit, and his worshipers must worship in the Spirit and in truth.
John 4:23–24, NIV

I couldn't help but worship Him. My heart of worship was being restored, and only God can do this. If we call unto Him, He will answer.

It led me to repent for not taking the time to worship Him because it is in worship we find Him and see Him. He reveals more of Himself to us.

Prayer...

God, You are the One who leads us to Yourself. Help us to be more aware when You're leading us to worship You and enable us to spend time with You. Cause our spirits and hearts to be in tune with Yours and to hear Your voice when You're calling us. Sometimes we can't hear because of all the busyness of our lives and everything that's going around us. May everything we do be an act of worship unto You.

Inner Beauty

Reflection...

1. What are some things you do on a daily basis that are acts of worship to God? Name some activities that are not.

2. What are some things you are willing to put aside to spend more time worshipping God? Here are some examples: TV, social media, hobbies, and work.

3. If you can't think of any, ask God to show you. He is faithful to show us if we are willing to listen.

Giving Thanks to God

Morning Devotional

It was Saturday morning, and it was sixty-one degrees in February. Yes, sixty-one degrees is unusual for February, but I was not complaining. It was a beautiful sunny day in Kansas City. I was sitting at the dining room table with the window open to let the fresh air in. I heard the train miles away and the birds chirping in my yard. I heard the neighbors sawing and probably working on outdoor projects. It was certainly a warm day for it, but I also sensed a quietness too. It felt so peaceful.

I thanked God for His goodness because only He can give us this peace. Sometimes we take so many of God's blessings for granted, such as being able to wake up to another day, to be able to walk, to talk, and to move around. I was thankful that I had a job to go to. I had friends I could call

Inner Beauty

and pray with. I had a roof over my head and food in the fridge to eat. I was thankful that I had a car to drive. I was thankful that my mom was still alive, and I could call and pray with her. I was thankful that my daughter and I had a relationship, and we could hang out. I was thankful that I had a Godly hardworking husband, who provides for us.

I was thinking of my friend, who had a stroke last summer and had not been able to take her walks like she used to. She would walk everywhere, and it ached her not to be able to do that right now, but she has faith in God that one day she will. She is recovering slowly, but she can move her legs and arms, and for that she is thankful. This is one of my friends I pray with at least once a week. She does not give up even though she can't just get up and walk to her favorite stores right now. Though she can't walk in the natural, she continues to walk out her salvation with fear and trembling. She is walking in faith in Spirit.[15]

If I ever get discouraged by not being able to do something or thinking I can't go on with life, I think about my friend Julie who continues walking by faith and not by sight. I am very grateful to God for her friendship. I have nothing to complain and murmur about, but only giving thanks to God.

> I thank my God every time I remember you.
> Philippians 1:3, NIV

> Rejoice in the Lord always. Again, I will say, rejoice!
> Philippians 4:4

Prayer...

Thank You, God, for all that You do for me. I thank You for every day that I wake up and grab my coffee to sit with You before I get ready to go to work. I thank You for providing a house, a car, a job, and food, these are things I take for granted sometimes. I thank You for my family and friends. I thank You for all the answered prayers and those I'm still waiting for to be answered.

I thank You that You sent Your Son, Jesus as a ransom to pay for my sin so that I can have eternal life and spend eternity with You, which is the greatest gift of all. Thank You, God, that You loved me that much. We give You thanks because You are worthy, God.

Reflection...

1. What are some things you are thankful for today?

2. What are some things you sometimes take for granted?

Challenge...

Write a list of everything God has done for you and all the prayers He has answered in your life.

God Won't Let Us Down

Summer

One summer evening while sitting in the living room, enjoying my solace and worshipping, I heard this phrase: "It's not in God's nature to let us down."

How profound. It's not in God's nature to let us down. It really got me to meditate on this phrase and pray: "God, remind me of this when I am tempted to worry about my circumstances. When I'm not seeing prayers being answered fast enough or the way I thought they would be answered because I had my own plans."

It's not in His nature. What does that mean? He always answers yes, no, wait, or He says, "I have something better."

I know He was asking me, "Do you want the better?"

Sometimes that better doesn't always include circumstances changing right away, but the better always includes Him to be priority. His Word says:

> Come, all you who are thirsty, come to the waters; and you who have no money, come, buy and eat! Come, buy wine and milk without money, and without cost.
>
> Isaiah 55:1, NIV

The better is something money can't buy. He asks because He knows us so well. He knows our flesh is weak. He knows we are prone to trust in man instead of putting our trust in Him.

What is His better? His better is His presence, His joy, His peace, and His love. Now these are things money can't buy, but we get them only by spending time with Him and reading His Word. Sometimes I forget how good it feels to be in His presence.

> You have made known to me the ways of life; You will make me full of joy in Your presence.
>
> Acts 2:28

In His nature there is kindness, hope, and unconditional love. In His nature there is unfailing love, abundant life, and supernatural grace.

"God, You are on Your throne, and You see all things, and You are confident and secure.

"You're the best. Your love is better than anything this world could offer. Though man and this world let us down and don't meet our needs, You will not let us down.

"You say we were not created to look to man or this world to satisfy us, but we were created with a longing only you can satisfy. If circumstances were perfect, we would not look to You."

God speaking to my heart: "If everything in your life were perfect, you would not look to Me. I know man very well. Man looks at the outward, but I look at the intent of the heart. Your mouth says one thing, but I know man's heart, and his heart is far from Me. They look to their own resources and to their own provision. They look to their own hands to provide for themselves. Look to Me, and seek Me while I may be found. Come unto Me. Come to the waters. Come into My presence, and there you will find love. I will satisfy your every need and your every desire that gives you life."

Prayer...

God, show us Your true nature. Help us to be confident and secure in You. Show us that You will not let us down. Give us a deeper revelation of who You are. Give us hearts to trust that You are faithful, holy, and perfect. You are worthy, and that's who You are. Show us the truth of who You really are and tear down the lies and misconceptions we have believed about You. You are not like man that You would lie. You have a good nature. You are good all the time. You are faithful. You are spirit, infinite, eternal, and unchangeable in Your being. You have wisdom and power. You are holiness, justice, goodness, and truth, and You love us.

Inner Beauty

Reflection...

1. What are some lies or misconceptions you have believed about God? If you don't know, ask God to show you.

2. What are some ways God has shown you His good nature? His faithfulness? His love?

Challenge...

Ask God to show you truth about His nature and to heal you of past woundedness that has kept you from believing who God really is.

Come to a Quiet Place

> [Jesus] said to them, "Come with me by yourselves to a quiet place and get some rest."
>
> Mark 6:31, NIV

It's five o'clock on Sunday morning, and I'm still in bed and wide awake. I'm thinking: "This is way too early to get up," and this is my work alarm going off, but I can feel God nudging me to get up. I go to straight to the kitchen to make me some dark-roasted coffee; I add a little vanilla creamer because the coffee is way too strong. I go to my usual place in the living room—the couch. By the corner of the couch there is a little side table where I have all my journals, calendar, and a pile of stuff, which is usually a mess, but not this morning because I had organized just the day before.

Inner Beauty

I open my Daily Bread booklet, which I enjoy most mornings when I don't have a lot of time. Today's reading is about taking time to rest. As I started reading it, at first I didn't think anything of it, but by the end of the passage I wondered if God was trying to tell me something. Of course, He was. If Jesus took time to go to a quiet place to rest and pray, then it is important for me to do the same.

Saturday and Sunday early mornings are probably the only two days when it is quiet, and I can spend quiet time with God. That's why God gets me up early because He knows once my husband gets up, I won't have that time. It is so quiet right now, it feels like time just sits still. No noise, just very peaceful. I miss these days when I can just sit and rest and listen to God.

Saturdays are always spent catching up with running errands or shopping because I am too tired from working all week. I look forward to Sundays because it's the only day I can really rest, and if God the Creator of the universe rested on the seventh day, then why shouldn't I? What better way than to be able to wake up and go sit in a quiet place with Him?

It feels so peaceful right now, and I am savoring this time. Resting is so good for the mind, body, and soul. It is refreshing; just like His Word nourishes our spirits and souls, rest and quietness refreshes our minds and bodies. It takes discipline to do this on our own, and sometimes we are forced to rest when we start getting sick.

I figured this out this past week. I had been on the go all week; by the end of the week I was feeling sick again. I was so upset because I had so many things to get done on the weekend. We were going to be busy purchasing another car and dropping off our old car we had just sold. My friend was coming out to visit from Texas, and I wanted to make sure I was going to be available to see her. By the end of this chaotic day, my husband and I picked up dinner and went to a park. I had been wanting to visit this little park that has a beautiful lake with ducks and a walking path. It looked so peaceful. We picked up Mexican dinner from one of our favorite restaurants and went to this little park, sat on a bench, and ate dinner while watching the sunset.

It was such a beautiful sunset with many beautiful colors of light pink, oranges, and reds. Sometimes we get so busy we forget to enjoy the simple things in life like just sitting by a lake and watching a beautiful sunset. It felt like a gift from God. We don't always get these days to just enjoy God's creation, but when we do I know it is a gift.

Prayer...

Thank You, God, for waking me up this morning to sit with You in a quiet place to rest. You know me better than I know myself, and You know what my body needs. You care so much about me that You send warnings because I miss the nudges to rest. Thank You for giving me this gift of rest and peace this morning. Help me to discern when my physical body needs rest and to obey when You call me to rest. Help me to realize that I can get more done when I get the proper rest and time with You than when I am too busy and tired. Thank You for giving us wisdom. Give us the grace to act on it. Selah and Amen!

Reflection...

1. Are you taking time to rest?
2. What are some things you can put on hold to take time to rest?

Challenge...

Take some time at home or go to a place where you can rest, read a book, pray, or just enjoy God's beauty and be in His presence. Take a walk by the beach, lake or park, or your backyard if you can't get away to talk with God; it will do wonders for you. Enjoy!

The Beauty of Journaling

Journaling can be one of the most rewarding things you can do. I enjoy it because it gives me peace when I write everything that's on my mind down on paper. I don't have to share anything. It's just me, my pen, and my journal. It helps me to release stress, all my worries, and what's on my heart.

I have been journaling for about twenty years. I keep many different journals for different uses. I use one for Bible study, one for prayers and answered prayers, one for writing notes for a book I am working on, and one for my everyday journaling.

Every new year I look forward to getting a new journal. My family knows that for Christmas I would like a new journal and a new pen, so I can write my new goals for the new year and a plan to help me accomplish them.

In fact, God encourages us to journal. I love this scripture in The Message version.

> And then GOD answered: "Write this. Write what you see. Write it out in big block letters so that it can be read on the run. This vision-message is a witness pointing to what's coming. It aches for the coming—it can hardly wait! And it doesn't lie. If it seems slow in coming, wait. It's on its way. It will come right on time.
>
> Habakkuk 2:2

One of my favorite things to do when I journal is to set the mood. I make a cup of organic mint tea or coffee in my favorite coffee mug—the one my daughter gave me for Mother's Day with pictures of her and me on it. I sometimes light a fire or a scented candle with some instrumental music playing. I don't always have the time to journal with such a relaxing atmosphere, but when I do get to, it is the most rewarding.

I love to encourage others to keep a journal, especially for the new year, so they can write their dreams, plans, and goals.

God wants us to dream big, so big that it takes God to fulfill them. God is supernatural and sometimes it takes a supernatural miracle for dreams to be fulfilled. It takes hard work and setting goals, but either way He gets the glory, not us.

He wants to make known His plans for us that are good and that will prosper us. I have seen visions and dreams in my life being fulfilled that could have only happened with

The Beauty of Journaling

God intervening. Moving from California to Kansas City, Missouri, was a dream being fulfilled. It took God's supernatural favor and intervening to bring this to a reality, and God is not a respecter of persons. He wants to do the same for all of us. It does take faith and trusting in Him that His way is better. God is not moved by our circumstances or limitations. He is moved by faith, because without faith it is impossible to please Him.

> Now without faith it is impossible to please God, for whoever comes to him must believe that he exists and that he rewards those who diligently search for him.
>
> Hebrews 11:6, ISV

Journaling can also be a way to communicate with God. Many times, when I am writing to God in my journal, God will give me answers to my problems through scripture. He will impress on my heart that everything is going to be OK and that I can put my hope and trust in Him.

One of the beauties of journaling is that it is so therapeutic for the soul and mind.

When I journal, it allows me to express my emotions on paper to God. When I let out my emotions and thoughts to God on paper instead of verbally, it allows an opportunity for Him to speak to my heart about what I am going through, especially when they are negative emotions tearing me apart.

I also like to keep my Bible with my journal in case God leads me to a scripture that will encourage me in whatever I am facing that day. God's Word gives me peace of mind and heals my soul especially when I have so many thoughts running through my head and emotions going through my heart.

Inner Beauty

This is what the Lord, the God of Israel says: "Write in a book all the words that I have spoken to you.
                              Jeremiah 30:2, NIV

Be encouraged today to enjoy the beauty of journaling.

Challenge...

Buy a journal with a favorite scripture, design, or color. (Walmart has very inexpensive journals you can purchase.) If you already have one and haven't had time to write in it, I challenge you to just take five to ten minutes every day just to reflect on your day. You might enjoy writing. Enjoy the beauty of journaling.

Tea with Little Ole Me

Late Fall

It was the end of fall. All the trees started looking bare, most of the leaves had already fallen. Thanksgiving was right around the corner. It was one of my favorite seasons in Missouri.

I was so excited because my friend Penny was coming for a visit to see her family, and she was going to stop by to spend some time with me. I hadn't seen her in about a year since she'd moved back to Texas. I planned to have a tea party for her because I knew she enjoyed them as much as I did.

I decorated the dining area with fall colors of bright oranges, reds, and yellows. I brought out all my teapots and teacups that were fall colored. I also brought out the new beautiful Tea Cart Trolley my daughter had given me for

Inner Beauty

Mother's Day. It was absolutely stunning. It was dark oak with gold trimming. It was an Italian 1950 Hollywood Regency Marquetry engraved flower designed.

To serve the tea and the meal, I used my Ascot Sheffield design reproduction by Community set.

For lunch, I made cucumber and cream cheese sandwiches, turkey sandwiches, and cheese and crackers. For dessert, I made blueberry and raspberry scones topped with whipped cream. For tea, I made ginger peach black tea and raspberry tea.

I love having tea parties. I enjoy that women can get together and fellowship and enjoy each other's company. I think women should get together more often to be able to encourage and pray for one another, to laugh, cry, and be transparent with one another. In fact, God encourages us to do so.

> Therefore, as God's chosen people, holy and dearly loved, clothe yourself with compassion, kindness, humility, gentleness and patience. Bear with each other and forgive one another if any of you has a grievance against someone. Forgive as the Lord forgave you. And over all these virtues put on love, which binds them all together in perfect unity.
>
> Colossians 3:12–14, NIV

Making Time for Tea

I also enjoy having tea with just one friend; it's more intimate. I know many of us have busy lives with kids and jobs, but it would be nice to get together with a friend or friends once a month.

Tea with Little Ole Me

Maybe you already do this with one of your friends or several friends, but for those that don't, I encourage you to do this. Have a cup of tea, open up, encourage one another, pray for one another for this can be the greatest source of love, healing, and joy.

Ways to Enjoy Tea

- Enjoy a cup of tea in the morning while reading your Bible or your favorite devotional.

- Share a spot of tea with friends.

    > A sweet friend refreshes the soul.
    > Proverbs 27:9, MSG

- Take tea on the go. You can enjoy a picnic tea outdoors with some iced lemon-mint tea and jam cookies.

- Relax with chamomile tea before bedtime.

    > For so He gives His beloved sleep.
    > Psalm 127:2

- Host a children's dress-up tea party. Use a child-size tea set, and serve lemonade and lots of goodies.

- Throw a bridal-shower tea party. Make a relaxing time for the bride to share her joy with friends.

- Here are some resources I have used to host tea parties and to enjoy a cup of tea on my quiet time:

Inner Beauty

1. *Victoria:* The Essential Tea Companion, Favorite Menus for Tea Parties and Celebrations

2. *Blessings for the Morning and the Evening* by Susie Larson

The Lessons of a Garden

> The Lord will bring about justice and praise in every nation on earth, like flowers blooming in a garden.
>
> Isaiah 61:11, CEV

What can you learn from having a garden? You sow seed and watch it grow. If you don't water it or take care of it, it dies. I think it's so spiritually symbolic with our spirit. If we don't water our souls with the Word and prayer, we die spiritually. We get spiritually cold. If we fertilize, water, and take care of our garden, it flourishes, and I think that's what God wants for us. He wants us to flourish and blossom into beautiful beings.

I know I have gone through seasons of flourishing and seasons of dying spiritually. We have to water and feed our spirits and our souls. God speaks to me so much through gardening.

Inner Beauty

I plant seeds, and then I get to enjoy the fruits of my labor. I get to enjoy the beauty of the flowers' and plants' colors and fragrances. I have been fortunate to have a beautiful garden with flowers I didn't plant and labor over, and I enjoy the ones I did get to plant.

Just like with Jesus, He paid a price for us so that we can enjoy God and His blessings. We get to enjoy freedom, joy, peace, and God's unconditional love.

We get to enjoy God and Jesus for an eternity that was paid on the cross through Jesus Christ. That is the goodness of God.

I appreciate when I plant flowers from seeds or bulbs and watch them grow, flourish, and blossom. I think God enjoys us the same way. He enjoys seeing us growing and blossoming into beautiful flowers, but we can't grow unless we water and feed our spirits and go through trials and testings.

We learn through failure and successes, and with both we come out winning. We see the goodness and faithfulness of God. We grow in our faith and trust Him more. We learn that His Word is like water that strengthens and encourages our spirit.

We also need the body of Christ to grow and mature. We were never meant to go through trials and testings alone. Trials and testing can be like the heat of the sun that will drain us if we're weak, but if we are rooted in the Word of God and in Christ, we will remain living and standing strong.

We must remain standing with God, His Word, and the body of Christ. Flowers don't just grow on their own; they need water, sun, fertilizer, pruning, and care, just like we do. We were created to flourish and blossom into the beauty of Christ, so we can show His righteousness to all nations.

The Lessons of a Garden

I have learned some things about gardening and reasons seeds fail to grow.

Seven Reasons Seeds Fail to Grow

1. Seeds are planted too deeply. As a rule of thumb, plant a seed no deeper than three times the diameter of the seed and follow directions. Sometimes I am so excited to just plant the flowers or seeds that I don't follow directions. Because I am not into the details like my husband, well, I get failed results.

2. The soil is not prepared well; using organic mulch or compost ensures success in your garden. (How many times have we wanted to jump into something new, a new job or project, and we are not prepared well, and we don't have the right tools we need to do a good job or project?)

3. The soil is either too hot or too cold; if the soil is too hot or too cold seeds may fail to germinate and grow properly. Patience—something I need still need to learn about gardening. Learning how to wait on perfect timing to garden is like waiting on God's perfect timing for an answered prayer or move.

4. Overwatering the soil; soil should be moistened and never continuously wet. When I didn't know anything about plants, I use to drown my plants with water or forget to water them, and the result was always death.

5. Birds and squirrels have taken the seed. Oh, am I familiar with this in my own garden? We have many squirrels, rabbits, and even deer in our yard, and when

these animals get to my seeds or eat my plants the war is on. We have to use rabbit and deer repellent to keep them away from our garden.

6. The seed quality is poor. Sometimes the packaged seeds are damaged because of exposure to bad weather conditions. This has been the case for me some seasons when planting gladiolus that have been packaged. We have planted twenty bulbs, and only ten took root, so I try to plant about thirty.

7. Problems with Transplanting seeds outdoors, which I have not tried to do because I am not experienced with this.

Some of My Favorite Annual Flowers

Spring: gladiolus

Summer: phlox, summer majesty hybrid mix and marigold

Fall: mums, petunias, and the coleus with vibrant colored leaves that range from ruby red and yellow to pink, orange and blends.

The Lessons of a Garden

Challenge...

If you love to garden, you will enjoy this. If you have never done any gardening and are afraid to, then I challenge you to try it at least once. Activity: start a small garden with vegetables or flowers. Here is a good resource to get started: www.commonsensehome.com. Have fun.

Go to the Countryside

A New Season, Springtime

I was once again outside enjoying the warm weather and all the beautiful flowers that are hanging outside my canopy. There are hanging baskets full of white and pink calibrachoas. I can smell the aroma of the purple lilacs, white petunias, and the white lily of the valleys, my favorite scented flowers. The white peonies are starting to bloom again. Two Rose of Sharon trees are also blooming and give me shade from the summer heat and a sweet aroma from the beautiful pink and white flowers when they are in full bloom.

Oh, how I love and enjoy my flowers.

I remembered that Jesus spoke over me that I was like a Rose of Sharon, like a lily of the valley, a sweet-smelling aroma to Him.

Inner Beauty

> I am a rose of Sharon, a lily of the vallyes. Like a lily among thorns is my darling among the young women.
> Song of Solomon 2:1–2, NIV

I got up and grabbed the watering can, and I walked around the water fountain to water my new purple hydrangeas. Tears welled up in my eyes just thinking that this could be my last season living in Kansas City. All the precious memories and encounters with Jesus I had in my garden started flashing back. Part of me felt ready for a new adventure, but I was also a bit saddened to leave my beautiful garden behind.

I cried out softly, "Jesus, I don't want to leave this beautiful garden, the beautiful encounters of Your love. I know that You have more for me. New encounters, new adventures and a new season—Jesus give me grace not to look at it as if saying goodbye, but to look forward and that You are taking me deeper and wider in my relationship with you.

I went back to sit under the canopy, and this worship song by Mercy/Vineyard came to mind, and I began to sing to the Lord Jesus, who is like honey on my lips. Over and over I sang to Him, "I love You."

After I stopped worshipping, I heard God speaking to my heart.

"Don't be afraid to move forward into the unknown. I will give you peace, and you will know which way to go. Will you trust Me and come away with Me? Will you say yes, My beloved? I will show you greater things you do not know. A deeper love you have not yet experienced. Will you say yes?

I answered, "Yes, I don't know what to expect the future holds for me, but I say yes, Jesus, I will come away with You to the countryside."

Go to the Countryside

Come, my beloved, let us go to the countryside, let us spend the night in the villages. Let us go early to the vineyards to see if the vines have budded, if their blossoms have opened, and if the pomegranates are in bloom—there I will give you my love. The mandrakes send out their fragrance, and at our door is every delicacy, both new and old, that I have stored up for you, my beloved.

Song of Solomon 7:11–13, NIV

Notes...

1. See 2 Corinthians 12:9.

2. "Body Image," Advameg, Inc., accessed February 12, 2019, http://www.humanillnesses.com/Behavioral-Health-A-Br/Body-Image.html.

3. "Our Research," Dove, accessed February 8,, 2019, http://www.dove.com/uk/stories/about-dove/our-research.html.

4. Lizette Borreli, "97% of Women Suffer Poor Body Image; Dissatisfying Job And Relationships May Be to Blame," IBT Media Inc., August 9, 2013, https://www.medicaldaily.com/97-women-suffer-poor-body-image-dissatisfying-job-and-relationships-may-be-blame-250039.

5. "Our Research," Dove.

6. "Self Image/Media Influences," Just Say Yes, accessed February 12, 2019, http://www.justsayyes.org/topics/self-image-media-influences/.

7. "Eating Disorder Statistics," Mirasol Recovery Centers, accessed February 8, 2019, https://www.mirasol.net/learning-center/eating-disorder-statistics.php.

Notes

8. "Eating Disorders Facts and Statistics," The Recovery Village, accessed February 7, 2019, https://www.therecoveryvillage.com/mental-health/eating-disorders/related/eating-disorder-statistics/#gref

9. "Teens & Body Image...Changing the World," Stage of Life LLC, accessed March 18, 2019, https://www.stageoflife.com/TeensandBodyImage.aspx https://www.ssc.wisc.edu/~jpiliavi/357/body-image.htm http://www.stageoflife.com/TeensandBodyImage.aspx

10. See Matthew 6:26.

11. "Northern cardinal," The Robinson Library accessed May 21, 2019, http://www.robinsonlibrary.com/science/zoology/birds/passeriformes/cardinal.htm

12. See Proverbs 17:9; 1 Peter 4:8.

13. See Isaiah 26:3.

14. Dictionary.com, s.v. "intercede," accessed March 17, 2019, https://www.dictionary.com/browse/intercede.

15. See 2 Corinthians 5:7.

About the Author

Isabel Perez-McCoy is a creative writer, a songstress, and a missionary intercessor. She is the author of *Kissed by the Bridegroom*, which was written using all of her personal journals. Her second book Inner Beauty, continues her journey from self-rejection to God's acceptance and love. Her message in *Inner Beauty* was written to inspire and challenge women, young and old to accept who they are in God and finding their inner beauty—to walk in freedom from self-rejection to love themselves as God loves them. Isabel lives in Kansas City with her husband and daughter.

You can read some of her inspirational blogs and hear her music at www.RavishedByHisBeauty.com.

Connect with Isabel

f @ISABELMCCOYINNERBEAUTY

🐦 @IsabelMcCoy10

📷 @isabelperezmccoy/

MORE BOOKS FROM EAR TO HEAR PUBLISHING & SHE PROCLAIMS IMPRINT

After This: Understanding the Process of Preparation that will Equip You for Your Kindgom Assignment by Author Madelyne Douglas

Dear Woman: Losing hope in the midst of chronic pain and finding it again (A memoir) by Author Chavos Buycks

Do you feel called to write a book? If the answer is yes, then Ear To Hear Publishing LLC might be able to help you. Visit our website for more information, complete the publishing assessment and connect in to our writer's group.

www.EartoHearBooks.com

www.ingramcontent.com/pod-product-compliance
Lightning Source LLC
Chambersburg PA
CBHW020655300426
44112CB00007B/390